TRICKY TRIBAL DISCOURSE

TRICKY TRIBAL DISCOURSE
The Poetry, Short Stories, and Fus Fixico Letters
of Creek Writer Alex Posey

Alexia Kosmider

University of Idaho Press
Moscow, Idaho
1998

Material in chapter 3 is taken from "Hedged in, Shut up, and Hidden from the World: Unveiling the Native and the Landscape in Alex Posey's Poetry," by Alexia Kosmider; copyright 1996, MELUS, the Society for the Study of the Multi-Ethnic Literature of the United States, used by permission. Permission to reprint the following is hereby gratefully acknowledged: University of New England Press for Joy Harjo, "Trickster," from *In Love and War* (Wesleyan University Press, 1990) and for Alexia Kosmider, "Reinventing Trickster: Creek Indian Alex Posey's *nom de plume* Chinnubbie Harjo" from *Tricksterism in the Turn-of-the-Century American Literature* (University Press of New England, 1994).

02 01 00 99 98 5 4 3 2 1

Library of Congress Cataloging-in-Publication Data

Kosmider, Alexia Maria.
    Tricky tribal discourse: the poetry, short stories, and Fus Fixico letters of Creek writer Alex Posey / Alexia Kosmider.
        p.   cm.
    Includes bibliographical references and index.
    ISBN 0-89301-201-7 (alk. paper)
    1. Posey, Alexander Lawrence, 1873–1908—Criticism and interpretation. 2. American literature—Indian authors—History and criticism.   3. Posey, Alexander Lawrence, 1873–1908—Influence.   4. American wit and humor—History and criticism.   5. Frontier and pioneer life in literature. 6. Indians of North America in literature.   7. Indian Territory—In literature. 8. Discourse analysis, Literary.   9. Creek Indians—Civilization.   10. West (U.S.)—In literature.   11. Trickster in literature.   I. Title.
PS2649.P55Z74   1998
811'.4—dc21   97-2337
                                                                                          CIP

Cover: Photograph of Alexander Posey in the Walter Ferguson Collection, Western History Collections, used courtesy of the University of Oklahoma Library.

In memory of my father,
John J. Kosmider
(1924–1996)

CONTENTS

Introduction • *1*

1 • **9**
Grafting the Land
The Remaking of Indian Territory

2 • **21**
Inscribing the Indian Landscape
Alex Posey, Charles Gibson, and Ora Eddleman Reed

3 • **33**
Circumventing Speech
Western Poetics and the Shaping of Indian Territories

4 • **51**
Reinventing Trickster
Posey's nom de plume, *Chinnubbie Harjo*

5 • **65**
Spitting Out the Stories
Retelling Creek Verbal Traditions

6 • **79**
The Birth of Hotgun, Toopafka Micco, and Other Notable Creek
Characters

7 • **93**
Coming Full Circle
Alex Posey and American Literature

Notes • *101*

Bibliography • *109*

Index • *113*

ACKNOWLEDGMENTS

My grandmother would have been the first to say that "real" cooking is improvising, combining ingredients that you may have handy in your fridge and adding something that you never thought would add to the taste of your dish. This book is like my grandmother's "down-home" cooking—it is the effort of many people stirring the pot, adding a pinch of this or that. I would like to thank Robert Lynch, Bruce Rosenberg, and Robert Schwegler for their help in the inception of this work. Josie Campbell offered pointed criticism, and her enthusiasm for Alex Posey and Native American literature was extremely important to me. I am also indebted to Elaine Craghead for her friendship and love, and for her readings of early and late drafts of this study.

For sending various material that enabled me to complete my research, I wish to extend my appreciation to the staff of the Oklahoma Historical Society. I am also grateful to the staff of the Western History Collections at the University of Oklahoma Library for permission to reprint the photograph of Alex Posey, which appears on the dust jacket. I would like to thank MELUS for granting permission to reprint an earlier version of chapter 3, which was published under the title "Hedged in, Shut up, and Hidden from the World: Unveiling the Native and the Landscape in Alex Posey's Poetry." Daniel F. Littlefield Jr. shared his expertise on Alex Posey: for that I am also grateful. Furthermore, road trips are good for the soul and were essential for this study. Thank you, Mom, for driving west with me to help me finish my research. Finally, thanks to my friend Marianne Messina for listening to endless talk about Alex Posey and Creek literature.

INTRODUCTION

A photograph of Alexander Posey sits on my desk that is piled high with notes and sundry books. Sometimes I find myself glancing over at this picture, puzzled by its meaning. I imagine Posey carefully placing himself in this pose—a young Alex, probably in his late twenties, looking dapper in his felt derby hat. He wears a dark tweed jacket, unbuttoned, revealing a buttoned white vest with a high-collared starched white shirt underneath. One hand he places in his trouser pocket, while the other dangles by his side.

Posey does not gaze at the camera but turns away, choosing to show his profile. His picture is arresting, resembling photographs that I have seen of Robert Burns, someone whom Posey greatly admired. Burns was located between two worlds, Scottish and English. We may speculate that Posey, a Creek Indian writer and poet, living in Indian Territory at the turn of the century, may have been trying in this photograph to emulate one of his favorite poets. Like Burns, Posey is situated between two worlds, Euroamerican and Indian. In this photograph, we may ask, does Posey want to erase his culture-boundedness, creating a new representation of self? But at the same time, he seems to create a vision that speaks of cultural conflict.

I try to imagine how Alex Posey must have wanted to be "seen" in this picture. Perhaps, in some way, his photograph is an important key to understanding his literary work. Posey writes to dispel stereotypical ideas about Indians, but he takes on some of the dominant culture's ideas and values. His photograph also may seem to suggest that it is possible to erase "culture," yet his "Indianness" surfaces. Posey tries to frame his world as he so desired, creating his own self-image, assuming a posture that attempts to speak of a Euroamerican world-view. This confrontation between Euroamerican and Creek cultures drives much of his literary work.

Posey mediates between two cultures. He lived in a bicultural world: his mother, Nancy Posey, was a full-blooded Creek of the Wind clan, and his father, Lewis Henderson "Hence" Posey, was of predominantly

Scot-Irish heritage, and spoke fluent Creek. In 1889, at the age of sixteen, Alex entered Bacone Indian University, in Bacone, Oklahoma, where he qualified for the second academic year, approximately equivalent to high school freshman status (Littlefield, *Posey*, 41). Established by the Baptist Church as college preparatory for Indians, Bacone Indian University offered a conventional but rigorous curriculum, including Latin, science, math, literature, civil government, music, and art.

Not only did Posey receive a liberal education, he also had the opportunity to write and publish articles for the school newspaper, the *B.I.U. Instructor*, a faculty newsletter designed to promote the good work of the institution (45). At B.I.U., Posey demonstrated his lifelong interest in Creek verbal traditions. He wrote down some of these stories, which were later published in the *Instructor*, through which he gained local notice for his literary efforts (45). During the academic year 1893–1894, he did some reporting for a local weekly newspaper, the *Eufaula Indian Journal*. His work included gossipy news columns about the students, faculty, and some of the more interesting visitors to the university, and he also wrote special-interest columns about campus events (54).

Alex Posey's writing is a journey through conflicting cultural representations. On the one hand, his writings, especially his short stories and his Fus Fixico letters, reflect his people's struggle against colonialism, giving substance, authenticity, and power to his work. His works also show the cultural forces at work in Indian Territory as he tries to negotiate dichotomous world-views. Although at times Posey takes on the stance of the dominant culture, his experience as "other" never really can be dissociated from his writings; instead, bicultural tension floats just beneath the surface, erupting without warning onto the page. However, tracing Posey's dissimilar beliefs about Indian identity and culture is difficult, since his works often contradict and sometimes collide with one another. In this constant vacillation, a kind of dual posture embodies the power of his work.

This book is thus an attempt to understand Posey's multiple and divergent voices—voices that evolved through experience, through his constant negotiation of his conflicted position. Posey develops his distinctive voice(s) when he incorporates specific elements, such as Creek and black dialects, verbal arts, and trickster figures, into his work, all of which are derived from Creek verbal tradition. To demonstrate that certain elemental details of Posey's art reflect this adaptation, I will present an evolutionary approach, investigating first his more striking replication of Western literary models and then proceeding to other writings that reflect his attempt to incorporate and/or reproduce Creek verbal elements and strategies into his works. As Posey carefully arranged himself in his photograph, creating a desired "pose" that emulates the stance of an erudite poet, he also attempted to arrange his writings to "look" like Euroamerican models. However, an examination of Posey's work through an evolutionary approach demonstrates that he was also influenced by the historical and cultural context of his world, Indian Territory. Of course, no individual writer or artist lives sealed away from his or her world. Similarly, Posey's work, especially his Fus Fixico letters, was influenced by the rapid changes that Indian Territory underwent during his lifetime. At times, as evidenced by his desire to rewrite Creek verbal art forms, Posey wanted to preserve such traditions; his inclusion of other elements of Creek verbal arts into Western literary forms also demonstrates that these traditions shaped the literary conventions that he adopted. Therefore, to establish these important connections, chapter 1 provides the cultural and historical framework for understanding the conflicted position of Posey as he resided in Indian Territory and also gives biographical information necessary to discuss Posey's work in detail. Chapter 2 situates Posey within the Indian literary tradition of his time, linking him with other Indian writers who also published in territorial newspapers and mainstream magazines. The remaining chapters examine his various literary writings: poetry, short stories, Creek stories, and his Fus Fixico letters.

Chapter 3 focuses on what I believe to be Posey's most conflicted writing, his poetry. His verse has been overlooked by almost every literary critic except Daniel Littlefield, who investigates his poetry in his biography *Alex Posey: Creek Poet, Journalist, and Humorist*. Littlefield situates Posey within the Indian landscape and links him with the Western poets who influenced his verse. One problem that Littlefield addresses is that Posey inserts *rill* and *brook* into his verse when he lives amid the hills and creeks of Indian Territory (121). This investigation of Posey's poetry goes beyond the appropriateness of word "usage" or the flatness of his language in his poems about Indians and Indian Territory. His poetry reflects his desire to formulate poems according to the conventions of writers such as Walt Whitman, Emily Dickinson, and Robert Burns, all of whom he avidly read during his college years. He attempted to negotiate a voice through the appropriation of model Western writers and their literary conventions. In this chapter Posey's ideals and beliefs about Indians are compared to

Thoreau's as a means to determine how Posey takes on Euroamerican attitudes and how he departs from Western models.

Two short stories, "Mose and Richard" and "Uncle Dick's Sow," are the focus of chapter 4. In these stories, Posey imitates black dialect and also relies on trickster-like strategies as he reveals dissimilar cultural codes that come into play in his complex and shifting world. His short stories mirror the realities of divergent cultural codes. Posey's texts disclose a medley of characters who at times speak candidly about otherness, but at other times simply hint at their marginalized position through their words or actions. Posey's stories also reveal the multiple and complicated position of otherness: sometimes his characters show sympathy toward blacks or Indians; more frequently, he shows Indians as opposite of blacks.

Chapter 5 examines Posey's "rewriting" of Creek verbal art as he transforms these stories onto the written page. He creates a new fiction in which Chinnubbie, Posey's own version of a trickster, recounts his peripatetic adventures and outsmarts Owl and his fellow tribes-people. Even though Posey espouses assimilationist policies of Indian reform, he simultaneously demonstrates that he does indeed appreciate the verbal traditions of his fellow Creeks.

Posey's Fus Fixico letters, which brought him notoriety in his own time, are examined in detail in chapter 6. Daniel Littlefield and the late scholar Carol Petty Hunter published all seventy-two of these letters in *The Fus Fixico Letters*. My analysis of Posey's Fus Fixico letters could not have been accomplished without the authors' meticulous contextualization of these letters. Littlefield and Hunter also provide a brief examination of Posey's use of Indian dialect humor and the influence of the American humorist tradition of Finely Peter Dunne, George Ade, and others on his work. However, I argue that Posey's Fus Fixico letters are not only his most distinctive form of writing but also, and more important, emerge from his sensitivity to Creek verbal traditions. The letters link Posey to his Creek heritage as Fus and his friends provide an Indian perspective on making sense out of the shifting political arena of their homeland as it becomes a hotbed for corruption and land fraud. Posey's full-blooded Creek characters are positioned around traditional storytelling events and capture the dynamic interplay of language games, including the "grunts" and "nods" of Wolf Warrior or Kono Harjo spitting in the ashes of the fire. These signs affirm what the speaker tells his audience and help sketch the speech event so that readers can practically see and hear the performance.

To seek an understanding of the adaptation and transformation of verbal art to written forms, I have relied heavily on a multitude of theoretical approaches in investigating Posey's divergent voices. I draw on the field of ethnopoetics, which primarily focuses on stylistic or formal elements that enhance meaning in verbal traditions (Finnegan, 44). Scholars (Tedlock, Hymes, Rothenberg, and Briggs) have devised new methods of transcribing and analyzing texts in an attempt to interpret the performative aspects of verbal art traditions (Briggs, 4). For example, a seminal work in the field, Dennis Tedlock's *Finding the Center: Narrative Poetry of the Zuni Indians* reproduces a text in a way that captures the storyteller's emphasis on specific words, the changes in the pace of the storyteller's delivery, and fluctuations in volume, and also notes other metalinguistic features. In other words, Tedlock's translation privileges the performative element of the verbal art, in a Zuni creation myth, by reproducing its varying aesthetic textures by means of typographical variations (Krupat, 129).

A related field, currently popular among American anthropologists and folklorists, the field of performance theory, informs my investigation. Similar to ethnopoetics, performative theory focuses on the performative event; it also stresses the importance of context "rather than on the supposedly enduring and a-social text or script" (Finnegan, 43). Richard Bauman states that performance is a mode of communication, "a way of speaking, the essence of which resides in the assumption of responsibility to an audience for a display of communication skill, highlighting the way in which communication is carried out, above and beyond its referential content" (Story, 3). Recently a number of writers have sought to redefine our understanding of the context as it relates to performance; they stress contextualization, which "involves an active process of negotiation in which participants reflexively examine the discourse as it is emerging, embedding assessments of its structure and significance in the speech itself" (Bauman and Briggs, 69). By reexamining and redeveloping the manner in which we conceptualize a performative event, researchers refer to the fluid nature of any particular speech act. Barbara Babcock's work has been especially useful in examining what she refers to as metanarrative elements, "those devices that comment upon the narrator, the narrating, and the narrative both as message and as code" (67). It is my belief that such research provides new possibilities for investigating verbal traditions and brings us closer to appreciating the multidimensional nature of verbal art forms.

In addition to these theoretical approaches, my analysis is informed by postcolonial literary theory. An important foundation for my analysis of otherness and difference is by Bill Ashcroft, Gareth Griffiths, and Helen Tiffin, *The Empire Writes Back*. Although this text fails to include Native American literature in its analysis, it does provide a framework to interrogate the convergence of Native cultures and languages with dominant Euroamerican cultures. Along with basic postcolonial theories of subjectivity, my work incorporates a broad range of theoretical perspectives, such as biographical, historical, and anthropological. Littlefield's *Posey* provides the biographical foundation for Posey's political beliefs and attitudes about Indians and Indian Territory. Another analytic core of my work lies in the theoretical perspectives of Roy Harvey Pearce, Brian Dippie, and Arnold Krupat. These authors provide important frameworks for understanding the nature of hegemonic relations and the manner in which nineteenth-century Euroamericans perceived Indian cultures. Specifically, Krupat's discussion of monologic and dialogic voices has clarified my own beliefs concerning Posey's multiple voices. A third major field that I draw upon to understand Posey and Creek verbal art forms is the field of ethnography. However, I realize the inherent problems of relying exclusively on such texts. When specific chapters include the documentation of ethnographic material, I also include texts collected by Native storytellers of both the Creek and the Cherokee Nation. I believe that this approach strengthens the theoretical failings of individual ethnographic collections in interpreting Native peoples' verbal art forms and thus presents a larger basis for understanding Creek culture and verbal traditions. Finally, in my literary analyses I generally present my own eclectically informed interpretations of Posey's stories, letters, and poems, given a lack of secondary material on these texts. Though I view the texts through a matrix of lenses, as historically and culturally specific as I have attempted to be, some of Posey's Native readers may have responded differently to his stories.

Posey's own writings, however, parallel similar interests: through his literary work, Creek verbal traditions live and are transformed. As a young boy, Posey was a willing audience for his mother, who was known for her ability to tell a good story. Posey listened to the wide array of stories about Opossum, Skunk, and the Creek trickster, Rabbit, as he bests larger and more ferocious animals.

Posey was drawn to the magic of these stories and the wit and humor that the various animals demonstrate. But he also understood how "talking" animals allow one to comment on the social and political events of the time; he therefore uses a verbal art strategy (metanarration) in having animals comment on peoples' lives, their desires, their follies, and their fears. Rabbit tricks his way through the thick brambles of the woods, outmaneuvering Wildcat, Opossum, and other animals, and he pokes his nose into every nook of society, even finding his own feces fascinating.

It is likely that Posey would have heard the story in which Rabbit brags to Man-eater (Lion) about his own "spectacular" excrement. In order to prove that his is better than Man-eater's, both sit down side by side, close their eyes, and defecate. Before Man-eater opens his eyes, however, Rabbit switches their feces; when Rabbit stands up, there is a huge pile of bone under him. Pleased, Rabbit announces: "This is my kind of excrement." When Man-eater looks behind him, he notices that his is different from what he remembers, and he exclaims: "That is not my kind at all—there is something wrong" (Swanton, *Myths*, 42). For Rabbit, nothing is left over-turned, so to speak. Rabbit's appetite for escapade, along with his propensity to scrutinize every ritual or practice imaginable, appealed to Posey, who would later apply this trickster-like tactic to his own characters in his short stories and Fus Fixico letters. Similar to scholars of performance theory who assert performance involves "an assumption of responsibility to an audience for a display of communicative competence" (Bauman, *Verbal Art,* 11), Posey's rewriting of Creek stories shows his ability to effectively reproduce competent performances. With the skill of a good story-teller, Posey "retells" and transforms these stories to the written page. Posey "writes" the language of animals and tricksters and, as a result, captures a deeper language, the essence of Creek culture. Simon Ortiz, Acoma poet and writer, states that the "oral tradition is not just speaking and listening" to a social group, but recounting the "whole process of that society in terms of its history, its culture, its language, its values, and subsequently its literature" (Coltelli, 104). In spite of Posey's tendency at times to adapt to the politics and beliefs of the dominant society, he recreates the tribal worldview of transformation and survival through his "rewriting" of Creek oral stories and his creation of his Creek characters Fus, Hotgun, Tookpafka Micco, and others. His particular proclivity to pay attention to the performative aspects of Creek verbal traditions and thereby "rewrite" their effects into his prose will be investigated in greater detail in the forthcoming chapters.

1

GRAFTING THE LAND
The Remaking of Indian Territory

Well, so the grafter he been here a long time and was a pioneer, like
the Dawes Commission. He was first come and sell the Injin light-
ning rod for dollar foot and run it all over the cabin and maybe so
stick it in the ground two three times for good measure.

Then the grafter come and sell the Injin steel range cook stoves
too big to get in the cabin and burn up too much wood. So the Injin
was had to build a brush harbor [sic] over it out in the yard and
let it rust.

Then the grafter he come 'long again with a big clock that was keep
time like a almanac and didn't had to be wound up till it run down.

Then the grafter he go through the country and sell Gale har-
rows too heavy for four mules to pull to Injins that didn't had
nothin to plant but a pint of sofky corn and a hill a sweet potatoes.

Then the buggy grafter come 'long and done business with the
Injin.

So everywhere you go now you find lightning rod for clothes line
and steel range cook stoves for the children's play house, and cal-
ender [sic] clocks for ornament over the fireplace and Gale harrows
for scrap iron and buggies for curiosities.
—Fus Fixico letter[1]

Posey's world and the focus of his writings, Indian Territory, became
the site of shifting boundaries as tribal people, largely from the
Southeast, relocated early in the nineteenth century to the eastern por-
tion of land in what is now the state of Oklahoma. Early on, before the
Indian Removal Act of 1830, tribes such as Senecas, Quapaws, Osages,
Shawnees, Choctaws, Creeks, and Cherokees voluntarily migrated, con-
vinced by various treaty agreements that this was a better alternative than
probable extermination. Joining the early inhabitants were numerous plains
and woodland tribes, creating a diversity of Indian culture not present in

any other state or territory (Strickland, 5). The Indian Removal Act forced other tribal peoples, such as the five southeastern nations,[2] to relocate from their homelands of Georgia, Alabama, and Florida during the 1830s. Hundreds made this long trek to Indian Territory, with more than one-fourth dying from exposure or exhaustion (4). Sometimes referred to as the Trail of Tears, this brutal forced-march made a permanent impression on survivors and their descendants.

Yet in spite of severe hardships, the five southeastern nations prospered in their new homeland. After removal from their tribal lands, many converted to Christianity. Only the Creeks briefly resisted the work of the missionaries.[3] Generally speaking, all five nations were receptive to Christianity, and their new-found religion became integral to their community gatherings (Debo, 7). Adaptation to Euroamerican society proceeded rapidly as the five nations borrowed from mainstream society while still preserving their own cultural traditions. The Creeks, along with the other southeastern nations, clearly recognized the importance of becoming literate. They quickly assimilated educational models that replicated white models. By the time Alex Posey was growing up in Indian Territory, the majority of Indians had had some rudimentary schooling; most could at least read or write.[4] Several tribal newspapers, such as the *Cherokee Phoenix* and the *Cherokee Advocate,* continued to be published throughout most of the tribal period, keeping Indian people well-informed about local and public issues.[5] The Choctaws and Creeks followed with their own newspapers, but they were less successful and had fewer Indian-owned newspapers than the Cherokees. The people of the five nations stressed literacy as well as education in general as an important consideration for tribal survival.

Each of the five southeastern nations maintained its own school system until 1899, when the secretary of interior appointed John D. Benedict as the superintendent of Indian schools for the Indian Territory (Debo, 66). Benedict's rather caustic evaluation of Indian schools indicates that he was uninformed about what had transpired in the territory before 1899. The superintendent, testifying before a federal investigator in 1903, said that "a great majority of the Indians could read and write, an achievement for which the [federally administered] schools must be given great credit" (67–68).

Benedict's most grievous mistake was his inability to understand the importance and the value that the various Indian nations placed on education. The tribal school system of the five southeastern nations predated by many years the school system in Benedict's home state of Illinois (68). Angie Debo points out that Benedict's patronizing stance must have incensed tribal people, who for many decades regarded their schools as "their highest creative achievement" (68). Benedict also failed to note that many Indian students, such as Alex Posey, were not only literate but also college-trained.

Along with their educational interests, the five southeastern tribes' governing systems, although differing from one another, resembled Euroamerican models. The Creeks, for example, comprised a confederation of various tribal peoples (mostly speaking the Muskogean languages), with the town as the basic political unit. After the Civil War, they drew up a national constitution and a code of civil and criminal law. Besides creating a new constitution, the Creeks formed a National Council, consisting of two houses—the House of Kings and the House of Warriors. Individual Creek towns chose their council members, based on Creek traditional systems of representation.

The five southeastern nations' emphasis on farming, along with their permanent villages, further connected them with Euroamerican models. According to Euroamerican nineteenth-century beliefs, the quintessential "civilized" person owned property, which he farmed. This image of the farmer eking out his existence as he tamed the wilderness became a dominant symbol of this era, epitomizing the promise of American life. Henry Nash Smith, in *Virgin Land,* writes about this agrarian myth of the small farmer as the backbone of civilization:

> The master symbol of the garden embraced a cluster of metaphors expressing fecundity, growth, increase, and blissful labor in the earth, all centering around the heroic figure of the idealized frontier farmer armed with the supreme agrarian weapon, the sacred plow. Although the idea of the garden of the world was relatively static . . . its role in expressing the assumptions and aspirations of a whole society and the hint of narrative content supplied by the central figure of the Western farmer give it much of the character of a myth. (123–24)

More than any other Native group residing in Indian Territory, the five nations mirrored Euroamerican agrarian systems. Like Euroamericans, many Indians became affluent landholders by leasing their lands to non-Indians for grazing, coal mining, or lumbering; some Indians hired others to work as sharecroppers on their farms (Grinde and Taylor, 217). In addition to the relatively small number of Indian farmers, there was an Indian plantation class that followed the agricultural pattern of large-scale southern plantation owners; like the southern planters, they owned slaves.

Before the Civil War, the five southeastern nations owned black slaves. After the war, freedmen lived in villages, often near their former owners. But at the close of the war, the Cherokees, Creeks, and Seminoles granted full citizenship to their former slaves (Debo, 10). It is probable that even when freed, these former slaves were regarded in a proprietary way. Perhaps the Indians perceived them, not so much as "other," but as affiliates of the tribe. This seems to be likely, especially when intermarriage was frequent among the two groups. Moreover, freedmen culturally resembled their former Indian owners: they spoke Indian languages and shared their foods and other customs and traditions (Grinde and Taylor, 214). Of course, there is no "monolithic" attitude among Indians toward blacks or any other group, as evidenced by the multiple positions that the members of the southeastern nations held concerning interracial relations. Because attitudes and beliefs about race varied considerably within Indian Territory, and because racial boundaries were not exacting, some individuals "crossed" racial lines. Blacks and Indians, especially the Seminoles and Creeks, intermingled freely until the 1890s. In contrast with the Cherokees, Choctaws, and Chickasaws, the Creeks and Seminoles had no laws against intermarriage between Indians and freedmen (216). For the most part, blacks and Indians cooperated with one another and eventually assimilated. Along with the possibilities of assimilation, however, the blurring of racial borders also brought problems such as "passing," loss of identity, and racial hostility. Some of these conflicts appear in Posey's writings as he tries to work out his own and his peoples' beliefs about interracial relations.

The level of acceptance and assimilation of freedmen varied among the five southeastern nations, with the Creeks and the Seminoles showing the most tolerance (214). By the 1870s, the majority of blacks within the Territory were the Indians' former slaves, but by the 1890s, many of the blacks came from neighboring states. Even though by the 1890s Euroamericans had become the dominant population of Indian Territory (in 1870, they were 3 percent of the total population; by 1890, 61 percent [217]), the Native groups were more distressed by the influx of "outside" blacks, frequently calling them "state negroes" to identify them as a racial group that threatened the status quo.

Native peoples as well as freedmen disliked these new immigrants, fearing that they would usurp political power and tribal lands, which had already diminished considerably after the Civil War (218). These "other blacks" coming into the territory were most likely perceived as aliens, and as a threat to borders (ideological, political, geographical, and sociological). Moreover, the fact that Euroamericans encouraged black emigration to the territory suggests they lumped people of color together as one group. Thus Native identities must have felt especially besieged. The attempt by the Oklahoma Immigration Association to encourage blacks to emigrate into the Oklahoma district fueled the fire for racial hostility. In the 1890s, Native peoples were antagonistic toward blacks.

The use of the territory as a release for political, class, or race conflicts is developed clearly in Smith's *Virgin Land*. A recurring theme in American history is that the western public domains would operate as a "safety valve" to keep economic and/or social strife from occurring in the more settled regions. In other words, when people suffered from poverty and/or unemployment, they could travel westward, becoming farmers. The *New York Tribune* of February 18, 1854, espoused this theory:

> Make the Public Lands free in quarter-sections to Actual Settlers and deny them to all others, and earth's landless millions will no longer be orphans and mendicants; they can work for the wealthy, relieved from the degrading terror of being turned adrift to starve. When employment fails or wages are inadequate, they may pack up and strike westward to enter upon the possession and culture of their own lands on the banks of the Wisconsin, the Des Moines, or the Platte, which have been patiently awaiting their advent since creation. Strikes to stand still will be glaringly absurd when every citizen is offered the alternative to work for others or for himself, as to him shall seem most advantageous. (Smith, 201–2)

Indian Territory became incorporated into the garden myth, enticing settlers, of European and African descent, to transform the "untouched" land into fertile farms. At the same time, it thus became the site of racial conflict among Indians, blacks, and Euroamericans. However, as we see racial relationships being played out in Posey's own writings, this conflict was not a constant and is itself conflicted in Posey's writings: at times he denigrates blacks, at other times he sympathizes with their position. Posey's beliefs about Indian, black, and Euroamerican relations reflect his own cultural, learned attitudes as well as the social interactions acted out in Indian Territory during his lifetime.

With the influx of more Euroamericans into the territory, the five southeastern nations struggled to hold on to their tribal domain, with conservative Indians resisting the portioning off of tribal land. It seemed inevitable that Indian lands would eventually be parceled out for Euroamerican investment and settlement: the myth of the garden appears in the idea of Indian allotment. The Dawes Act (1887) provided for allotting land in severalty to tribal members but exempted in its provisions the Cherokee, Creek, Choctaw, Chickasaw, and Seminole tribes. For a moment, at least, Congress did not interfere with tribal affairs. However, Indian Territory was becoming desirous to various Euroamericans, including railroad entrepreneurs, farmers, and ambitious politicians, who wanted tribal lands to be divided into individual parcels (Dippie, 244).

In 1893, Congress created the Dawes Commission to negotiate allotment agreements specifically with the Creeks, Choctaws, Chickasaws, Seminoles, and Cherokees—the five southeastern nations. Many Creeks were outraged with the Dawes Commission and its subsequent enactment of measures that spurred fragmentation within the Creek community. A well-known Creek businessman and public figure, George W. Grayson, wrote that his fellow Creeks were "paralyzed for a time [by] its bold effrontery" (M. Green, 102). For many years the Indians had witnessed a gradual but continual shrinkage of tribal lands as homesteaders and railroad companies whittled away at their domain. Furthermore, private land ownership runs counter to the Creek belief that land belongs to people collectively. Many Creeks developed a "horror of land cessions" (Debo, 32).

Regardless of the opinions and beliefs of Native peoples, the passage of the Curtis Act (1898) gave power to the Dawes Commission to conclude its business of completing tribal rolls so that individual land parcels could be handed out. At the same time, tribal autonomy was terminated (Dippie, 247; M. Green, 102–103). The government therefore enacted the long-threatened legislation, tribal tenure, that many Indians had feared (Debo, 33). After refusing to make a treaty with the government, the Creeks finally decided to honor the agreement, which was ratified by the tribe on May 25, 1901. Pleasant Porter, Creek tribal chief, recounts his peoples' predicament, stating that they had little choice but to accept the terms of the settlement. After the tribal leaders deliberated, they surrendered; Porter accepted the position of chief so that he could implement the agreement by influencing other, more obstinate Creeks to cooperate with the federal government (33). But Porter, like many Creeks, noted that Creek life would never be the same: "I will tell you . . . I have said that I was conscious that I was compelled under the advance of civilization to sign the paper now that I know [that I now know] took the lifeblood of my people" (33–34).

The majority of the Creeks submitted to the Dawes Commission's demands (M. Green, 104). Some, like Porter, thought that these changes were both negative and inevitable. Others, like Posey, were convinced that the changes enacted by the Dawes Commission would be beneficial. Posey believed that the best way for Indians residing in the territory to improve their condition was to accept allotment—this, he thought, should be accomplished for the sake of "progress." His view was not much different from that of the majority of Euroamericans; he did not really want Indians to "vanish," but he advocated a new lifestyle, modeled after mainstream values and beliefs.

Even as a relatively young man, Posey had been actively involved in the Creek Nation's political affairs. When he finished school at Bacone Indian University, he returned to tribal activities, holding various positions. In 1895, at the age of twenty-two, he served as a representative in the Creek House of Warriors, the lower house of the Creek National Council, representing his tribal town of Tuskegee (Littlefield, *Posey*, 5). The following year, Posey was appointed superintendent of the Creek Nation Orphan Asylum at Okmulgee. He held that post until 1897, when he resigned (Challacombe, 1014). In 1899, he served as the superintendent of the Eufaula boarding school and the following year as the superintendent of the National School at Wetumka (Littlefield, *Posey*, 5–6).

After owning, and writing editorials for, two territorial newspapers, the *Eufaula Indian Journal* and, later, the *Muskogee (Okla.) Times*, Posey reentered Creek tribal politics; this time he was employed as a fieldworker for the Dawes Commission, from March 1904 until February 1907 (225). One of Posey's jobs for the commission was to locate Creeks and persuade them to sign the tribal roll so they could qualify for their land allotment. He tried to enroll the so-called "lost Creeks" (Indians living in other Indian nations) and members of the Snake Faction, a group of discordant full-blooded Creeks who wanted to live their lives in the old way and who opposed allotment of tribal lands and the termination of tribal government. As a result of his position on the enrollment field party, Posey made contact with many traditional Creeks, such as Chitto Harjo (Crazy Snake), a leader of the Snake Faction.

Chitto Harjo was arrested in spring 1901 and later jailed for his role in trying to "undermine" the federal government. Posey's poem "On the Capture and Imprisonment of Crazy Snake" describes Chitto Harjo as a fearless leader:

> Down with him! bind him fast!
>   Slam to the iron door and turn the key!
> The one true Creek, perhaps the last
>   To dare declare, "You have wronged me!"
> Suffers imprisonment!
>
> (M. Posey, 207)

Even though, as this poem indicates, Posey became more informed and sensitive to Crazy Snake's perspective, he continued to espouse the belief that Indians "were relics of a bygone civilization who would be unable to participate in the political and economical progress of the twentieth century" if they did not accept allotment (Littlefield, *Posey*, 6). Posey, like most of the Euroamericans, failed to be sensitive to Indians, especially those he felt were traditional and maintained ideas that did not mesh with modern, mainstream society. In the same poem, he describes Crazy Snake as one of those "old-fashioned Indians":

> Such coarse, black hair! such eagle eye!
>   Such stately mien!—how arrow straight!
> Such will; such courage to defy
>   The powerful makers of his fate.
>
> (207)

As Posey narrates Crazy Snake's story of conspiracy, he paradoxically brings forth a silenced Creek voice: Crazy Snake's actions challenge Euroamerican ideology. Posey celebrates cultural difference by focusing on Crazy Snake's "coarse, black hair" and his "eagle eye." Yet like many Euroamericans, Posey reveals his tendency to romanticize Indians as he speaks about Crazy Snake's "stoic" stance. "On the Capture and Imprisonment of Crazy Snake" aptly demonstrates, as James Ruppert states, "not just a middle ground or an alternation" between two divergent views, but a syncretism of oppositional world perspectives (213). This stance epitomizes Posey's political and social perspective. Posey advocates allotment on the one hand, and on the other he admires Crazy Snake for what he must have viewed as a "last stand" that was as "crazy" as Custer's. Posey brings together two worlds, revealing his own bicultural tension at work in this particular poem.

In spite of this Snake Uprising, the majority of Creeks submitted to the Dawes Commission's demands (M. Green, 104). Some Indians, like Creeks who attended the missionary schools and other Euroamerican institutions, were convinced that changes in traditional Creek lifestyles would improve the economic conditions of their fellow Creeks. Others, like Chitto Harjo and his followers, accustomed to a traditionally-based Indian lifestyle, objected to assimilating Euroamerican economic and social institutional systems. Even Posey, who had spent time visiting many traditional Creeks and their families in their secluded homes in the back country while he worked for the Dawes Commission, still maintained the belief that the changes enacted by the Dawes Commission would be beneficial. In fact, Posey favored allotment so strongly that he wrote, "Indians if you ignore the opportunity which has presented itself to you in the shadow of an imminent peril, and which if you should accept, would place you where all that pertains to your welfare would have you, you will be guilty of wrongs and grievances to your prosperity." He pleaded that the Dawes Commission truly had the Indians' interest at heart, desiring to place them "in harmony with advancement of the world" (Littlefield, *Posey*, 75).

In 1889, the first of a series of land runs opened up tribal lands to Euroamerican settlement, which brought many facets of Indian life to a head. Until then, all land in Indian Territory, even though subject to federal regulation, had belonged to Indians (Strickland, 33). Thus, Euroamerican settlers on that land were on Indian domain and were subject to the same regulation. Eventually, though, Indians became victims as a struggle for political power and land refashioned Indian Territory into a contest between Indians and Euroamericans. Strickland notes, "These sovereign Indian nations were the only groups in Oklahoma whose political power and landed estate would diminish with the establishment of territorial government that had begun in 1889 and culminated with the admission of Oklahoma to statehood in 1907" (34). Political alliances shifted while land grafters seized tribal land.

The volatile Indian Territory landscape became the focus of many peoples' fears and interests. While controversy over large land schemers and railroad investors captured headlines in major eastern cities' newspapers, such news also launched Posey's career in journalism as he became a nationally recognized literary figure. From 1902 until his death in May 1908, Posey wrote seventy-two Fus Fixico letters—letters recounting "Fus" and his fellow full-blooded Creeks' humorous and sometimes caustic insights into events occurring in Indian Territory. In 1902, Posey bought the *Eufaula Indian Journal,* where some of his Fus Fixico letters appeared occasionally, and he served as editor of that newspaper for one and a half years (Littlefield, *Posey,* 6). Posey's humorous journalistic style created national interest; the *New York Times,* for example, characterized Posey's daily newspaper as "the latest novelty," stating that he was "one of the most prominent and influential men in the Territory."[6] Along with giving a detailed biography about Posey, the *New York Times* reprinted a sample Fus Fixico letter. Other articles about Posey, as well as his Fus Fixico letters, appeared in various newspapers, making him popular throughout the United States, Canada, and England.[7] In October 1903, Posey sold the *Journal;* he and a business partner purchased the daily *Muskogee Times,* and Posey became city editor.

Fus and his friends—Hotgun, Tookpafka Micco, Wolf Warrior, and Kono Harjo, all full-blooded Creeks—provide a lively commentary on territorial political dealings, sometimes focusing on the allotment of land or critiquing the shady dealings of one of the local politicians, as they smoke their pipes and spit into the fire. Sometimes Posey exposes the dealings of politicians, and at other times he sides with them. Indeed, it is his constant vacillation between wanting to be "Indian" and desiring to be "modern" that makes him a fascinating literary figure. Posey, along with other Native American writers, became a strong voice in the political struggle for land, power, and domination.

Since his early years as a student at Bacone Indian University, Posey embraced the dominant society's ideas of political, social, and economic progress (Littlefield, *Posey,* 139). But Posey also had close contact with conservative Creeks, like Chitto Harjo; sometimes he even sympathized with their position. Still, he felt that these Indians were "impediments to progress or unfortunate by-products of a changing social order" (9). At times Posey appears to share the prevailing Euroamerican view about the "progress" of his fellow Creeks. As Roy Harvey Pearce points out in *Savagism and Civilization: A Study of the Indian and the American Mind,* many Euroamericans viewed Indians paradoxically: they felt sympathy with their position but believed their extinction was inevitable (64). Walt

Whitman, whom Posey read and appreciated, prophetically spelled out the paradox, as he asked what seems unanswerable: who embodies the American Indian?

> The friendly and flowing savage, who is he?
> Is he waiting for civilization, or past it and mastering it?
>
> Is he some Southwesterner, rais'd out-doors? Is he Kanadian?
> Is he from the Mississippi country? Iowa, Oregon, California?
> The mountains? prairie-life, bush-life? or sailor from the sea?
>
> Wherever he goes men and women accept and desire him,
> They desire he should like them, touch them, speak to them, stay
> with them.
>
> ("Song of Myself" 976–83)

Even though Whitman fails to illuminate a thorough understanding of Indians, he does touch upon a Euroamerican mythic nerve, noting that Euroamericans "accept" Indians because they have become the mysterious "others." Thus as Euroamericans absorb Indians, they want to be justified. Euroamericans have it all—a "friendly" Indian in a pure state of nature. In other words, the Indian represents a romantic notion of the Indian's primitivism. Of course, Whitman fails to take into account how Indians react to being the object of Euroamerican desire. Unfortunately, they do not have a choice in this matter. Thus the Indian's desirous qualities as "other" are the manner in which nineteenth-century American culture built its own sense of Euroamerican-ness. American civilization "invented itself as the obverse or opposite of Native American 'savagism' what *we* would be, defined in relation to what *they* presumably were—or sensibly were not and could not be" (Krupat, 71).

This desire seems to embody or justify in some way the conquest of Native peoples and the seizing of tribal land to make a unified America. The American Indian is spun out of mainstream America's imagination, appropriated for Euroamericans' own use; *Indian* thus bears no relationship to anything resembling an accurate portrayal of a "real" Indian. Instead, *Indian* represents a complex cultural grid on which various complicated representations intersect and overlap. Such depictions as the "good" or "bad" Indian and the "Noble Savage" not only reflected but helped to shape Euroamericans' ideological beliefs and attitudes about Native peoples. Based on misrepresentation, ignorance, fear, and other phobias, Indians were marginalized socially, economically, and politically. Otherness is thus crucial to defining, and therefore differentiating, Euroamericans from Indians.

Nineteenth-century Euroamerican ideas about Indians were constructed by specific cultural codes regarding how Indians should be viewed. Alex Posey at times emulates the dominant culture's belief; at other times he celebrates and tries to dispel negative Indian stereotypes. His vacillation is the act of an individual who has difficulty understanding who he is— and perhaps accepting his Indian identity. Posey's struggle reveals the difficulty of mediating between two world-views.

2

INSCRIBING THE INDIAN LANDSCAPE
Alex Posey, Charles Gibson, and Ora Eddleman Reed

When the Lord first made man (of all colors) they were all one peo-
ple, [so] that the Lord offered them a choice, showing a piece of
paper first to the red man and he could make nothing of it and let
it alone, and the red man going along he found some roots and some
bows and arrows and he said these are mine, and so he lived in the
woods by roots and hunting.
    The white man then he looked at the paper and he could use it
and he kept it ("and how about the black people?"). There was
nothing said about them. . . . He said, referring to the white paper
which the white man took, that if he could have the chance he would
have taken the paper and then perhaps the Indians would have
everything as the whites have.
                           —*Creek (Tukabahchee)*[1]

Posey was not a solitary individual writing about the Indian landscape and
the political dealings of the white politicians vying for power in Indian
Territory. Contrary to what most people think, Indian territorial writers
tried to write themselves out from under the multiple misconceptions that
Euroamerican culture formulated and perpetuated regarding Indians
living in Indian Territory. This chapter situates Posey within the literary
tradition of his time, linking him with other Indian writers who also pub-
lished in various territorial newspapers and mainstream magazines. Posey
converses with Charles Gibson, a Creek writer, and Ora Eddleman Reed,
Cherokee owner of the *Twin Territories,* a prominent magazine of Indian
Territory. Posey, Gibson, and Eddleman Reed form a close-knit literary
community as they encourage each other's literary efforts as well as provide
an appropriate forum to counter the negative and derogatory beliefs about
Native peoples.
    Like Posey, Gibson, Eddleman Reed, and other lesser-known Indian
authors and poets recognized that Euroamericans harbored vastly

incorrect and, moreover, derogatory Indian images. Like Posey, Gibson and Eddleman Reed confronted negative Indian stereotypes, refashioning their own and Euroamericans' beliefs about Indian people. Their individual desires to write about their own perceptions about Indians and Indian Territory link these writers and illustrate a condition common to all Native peoples. Simon Ortiz, a renowned contemporary Indian poet and writer, asserts that the colonial experience drives much of Native American literature, since it is the social foundation that writers react against as they try to formulate alternative meanings of their own subjectivities by redefining their Indian identities and community experiences. The struggle to maintain cultural integrity and the resistance against losses—such as the prohibition on practicing religious beliefs or performing Native dances, or the divestiture of tribal lands—are exemplified in the writings of Posey, Gibson, and Eddleman Reed. Their voices resound collectively, speaking to one another in various territorial newspapers and magazines, signifying on each other's writerly talk. This chapter focuses on Posey's fellow Indian writers and demonstrates that a vibrant community of Indian territorial writers achieved powerful literary voices, voices that "rewrote" their own Indian histories and lives.

In 1902, Posey purchased the *Eufaula Indian Journal*, a weekly newspaper, with the idea that he would focus more on local rather than national or international news. In a sense, he envisioned his paper representing the "heartbeat" of the Creek Nation, since he believed that Eufaula would be the "coming city" in Indian Territory. Posey, as previously noted, embraced progress and believed his hometown would grow rapidly.

Several months later, Posey merged the *Indian Journal* with another local newspaper, the *Eufaula Gazette*. He promised his readers that he would continue to cover all public events in a fair and forthright manner: "We shall be satisfied to extend fair treatment to all, to publish the news and to go to our length in up-building of Eufaula, to us the only town in the wide world" (Littlefield, *Posey,* 140).

Along with the several weekly columns covering local events in the surrounding small towns of Bald Hill, Stidham, Fame, Lenna, and Canadian, Posey published a column, entitled "Rifle Shots," written by his close friend Charles Gibson. This column became a regular feature of the *Indian Journal* and was usually situated on the lower half of the front page, with the words *Horse Sense* and *Humor* appearing on either side of the headline "Gibson's Rifle Shots." Sometimes writing amusing stories, other times covering issues relevant to a specific political event, occasionally illuminating an old Creek tradition, Gibson's "shots" became one of the paper's mainstays, since the column attracted a wide circle of admiring readers. Gibson, born twenty-seven years before Posey, obtained what little formal education he had in the common schools of the Creek Nation and at Asbury mission.[2] Unlike Posey, who had the advantage of the rigorous studies at Bacone Indian University, Gibson did not have an extensive education. One local magazine characterizes Gibson as a "self-made man" because his education was so meager "that it can be said he is practically uneducated" (*Twin Territories*, July 1903). But still Gibson was widely recognized throughout the territory as a good storyteller, becoming "one of the best newspaper and short story writers among the Indians" (*Twin Territories*, July 1903).

Very few of Gibson's "Rifle Shots" are available for examination, but it is still possible to obtain some sense of the general thrust of his column. He was, as one reporter described him, "an old timer and an Indian of modern views" (Barnett, 37). In early 1903, Gibson, a full-blooded Creek, vehemently criticized the Dawes Commission's mismanagement of Indian land allotment, and along with George W. Grayson, another Creek writer and friend of Posey's, urged Indians to take their allotments so surplus land could not be further isolated from the Creek Nation and sold to speculators (Littlefield, *Posey*, 174–75).

Gibson wrote about the legendary history of the Spokegees (a faction of the Creek), who have been described as "somewhat slow and densely ignorant," a real "detriment to civilization" (*Indian Journal*, July 25, 1902). He explained that the "Spokegees" killed an early Creek leader for selling Indian lands to the U.S. government (Wright, 240; D. Green, 60). Gibson proclaims that he was a "genuine Is-Spo-Ko-Kee, on account of the Is-Spo-Ko-Kee blood in his veins" (*Twin Territories*, March 1901). Although Gibson kept informed about the political situation in Indian Territory, he was still interested in his Creek roots, writing about Creek lore and tradition whenever he had the opportunity.

Advocating the need to remember Creek history and tradition, Gibson showed empathy for the Creek Indians who were relocated to Indian Territory during the Removal of 1830. In one "Rifle Shots," he recounts a conversation with an old Indian lady, the last member of the McIntosh family to make the long trek from Alabama to Oklahoma. She said that "the government promised to pay the Creek for losses incident to their removal from the old country, but the promise has never been fulfilled and I am still expecting to receive pay some day for the great misfortune sustained by my family" (Barnett, 38). It appears that Gibson's "stories" were told for a real political purpose, given his stance on the Dawes Act. Gibson's "Rifle Shots" brought to the foreground many Creek family stories, including stories about removal.

Like Posey, Gibson writes in his column about changes occurring in Indian Territory and sympathizes with Creeks losing their land. In contrast to Posey, he resists rapid economic and political changes, especially detesting the gradual divestment of Creek land and the subsequent defrauding of Creeks by the government. Gibson voices his skepticism about the numerous injustices that he witnesses: "When a white man seems to be real good to you is a time for you to let him alone; he wants something real bad" (38). Gibson is more open and forthright in his approach to politics than is Posey, who uses other figures to espouse political views.

Gibson signifies upon Posey's Fus Fixico letters as Hotgun and his friends write out their wills, since it seems that their land allotments have been revoked by the government. One can readily witness how fiction mimics incidents actually occurring in the Creek Nation. Gibson writes: "Hot Gun, Tokpafka [*sic*] Micco and Kono Harjo have about decided to have their wills written, since Uncle Sam has made up his mind that they haven't enough in their sun-burned gourds to take care of themselves or of what belongs to them. Neither of them has any offsprings and will be compelled to will his old filly and windsplitter sow to some half step uncle or aunt" (*Indian Journal*, May 1, 1900). Gibson shoots off his rifle as he vehemently satirizes the government's policy of restricting full-blooded Indians, like Hotgun, from selling their land.[3] Hotgun, Tookpafka Micco, and Kono Harjo's situation leads Gibson to espouse his beliefs about allotment:

> And this leads us to think that is pretty tough on the red man, who once owned all the land between the Atlantic and Pacific. He has been shoved upon a little plot of dirt of one hundred and sixty acres and is told that he is too ignorant to do as he wished with it. This is not all. He has a surplus of many thousand acres of land which is withheld from his new born papoose which has a right

to an allotment as long as there is a foot of Creek domain left.
(*Indian Journal*, May 1, 1900)

This controversy probably helped the *Indian Journal* sell more papers, especially because of the columns that spoke to one another in this way. In spite of Gibson and Posey's philosophical differences concerning land allotment and assimilation, they were powerful political voices. The Creeks, as well as other Native peoples and certainly many white politicians, knew that Posey and Gibson could reach a wide audience. Both obviously understood their roles as influential literary voices within the territory as they sought to reaffirm each other's voice. Posey, with perhaps some genuine fondness, frequently refers to Gibson's "Rifle Shots" in his Fus Fixico letters. Fus appears to have had Gibson's "Rifle Shots" perpetually on his mind as he contemplates Gibson's humorous opinions or caustic "takes" on a given incident.

Sometimes Gibson's "Rifle Shots" even inspires Fus to write some more "news." Fus tells us: "Please, you must tell Charley Gibson that I was read what he says in the *Journal* last week about a dozen time. He told the truth good that time sure enough. Maybe so next time I write you more news to put in like this one" (Littlefield and Hunter, *Fus,* 54). Posey reaffirms Gibson's views while his comment persuades his own readers to read Gibson's "Rifle Shots." Posey tries to stand on both sides of the fence, supporting Gibson through Fus's letters while maintaining his integrity as editor and putting his political opinions aside. In another Fus Fixico letter, Gibson's "Rifle Shots" explodes into Fus's world. The specific article that Fus refers to is not certain, but nevertheless we know that he reads Gibson's column rather diligently. Fus says, "So I think big Injin chiefs was just want full-blood to turn grind stone so they could whet they old bone ax on it, like Charley Gibson say when he was shot his rifle off" (79). Again, Fus agrees with Gibson's opinion and lets his own readers know that they should also listen.

In another Fus Fixico letter, Posey lets his readers know who he listens to, reaffirming that Gibson's voice is important and sometimes paradoxically attempting to undermine it. Hotgun, with his customary forceful opinions, questions Tookpafka Micco about the Creek Union party's nomination of former chief Legus Perryman to be the last Creek principal chief. Many Creeks favored George Grayson, Posey's long-time friend, and Grayson's overturn created commotion within the Creek Nation.[4] Hotgun wants to know how Gibson reacted to "the big fight over the last bone," so he asks Tookpafka Micco: "Well, so what about Charley Gibson? And Tookpafka Micco say, Well, so he was load his rifle and say nothing" (110).[5] Here, Posey makes it clear that Gibson's rifle sometimes shoots blanks.

Gibson signifies on Hotgun, espousing his sentiments about land divestment; he also keys the reader to his own "hold" on words. Not only does Gibson want the white man to release Creek lands, but he signifies on a "white man" using "Indian language," "este charte," sometimes called "Red English." According to Littlefield, many other territorial Indian writers wrote in este charte.[6] Some of its characteristics are misspellings, a specific vocabulary, grammatical structure, and syntax (27).

Gibson tells his readers:

> Wouldn't that cork you and freckle your feet, too? We mean that white man trying to write este charte English in the Checotah thumb paper. It's the poorest dialect stuff that was ever forced upon the reading public. Don't dodge behind "Este Charte," white man, but get up your rot in straight English, if you can write it. (*Indian Journal,* May 1, 1900)

Gibson weaves a complete circle around este charte, making certain that he clearly demarcates the boundary between este charte and "white" English; he tells this white "Indian"-speaking editor: "Get from behind 'Este Charte' and wash the paint off your pale face. Take off the turkey feathers. They don't become you" (*Indian Journal,* May 1, 1900). Here, Gibson literally shoots apart a prevalent Indian image, forcing the white editor to unmask, while he strips him of his "turkey feathers" and his "paint," and makes him "spit" out his Indian words. What remains is a naked white man without speech. Gibson signifies on the white editor, underscoring the action of white men divesting the Indian of his tribal lands.

Posey, here politically allied with Gibson, reprimands the white man for appropriating este charte, declaring that the editor's language is a "fake": "Those cigar store Indian dialect stories being published in the Checotah papers and the Hoffman Herald Auxiliary will fool no one who has lived 'six months in the precinct.' Like the wooden aborigine, they are the product of a white man's factory, and bear no resemblance to the real article" (Littlefield and Hunter, *Fus,* 17). Posey calls attention to derogatory Indian images such as the "cigar store Indian," asserting that these images manufactured by white men are facsimiles, *not* the "real thing."

Posey and Gibson believe that to speak este charte is therefore to be a "real Indian," which cannot be duplicated by "outsiders." In a sense, they insinuate that este charte is the essence of "real" Indian language. Gibson warns the white editor: " 'Este Charte,' don't let that make you gay; for it will not be sale as real estate will be in Checotah" (*Indian Journal,* May 1, 1900). According to both men, este charte preserves Indianness, since it cannot be mimicked by others.

Eddleman Reed, like Posey and Gibson, addresses derogatory Indian images in her column, "What the Curious Want to Know," which appeared as a regular feature in *Twin Territories* (subtitled "The Indian Magazine"), published at Muskogee and Fort Gibson, Indian Territory.[7] Posey found *Twin Territories* promising, and through his *Journal* he praised Eddleman Reed's writing and urged people to subscribe to her publication. In turn, Eddleman Reed highlighted many Indian authors and poets in her magazine, among them Posey and Gibson. Her subscribers inquired about various Indian authors, especially about Posey. Eddleman Reed answered them:

> Biographical requests have been received for more information on the Indian writers, requests from all over have been received. Chinnubbie Harjo, whose poems and droll sketches have regularly delighted the readers of this magazine, should receive foremost attention. Chinnubbie Harjo is no other than the young and brilliant Creek Indian man, Mr. Alex Posey. (Morrison, 144)

Her political strategies for correcting misrepresentations of Indians, however, differ from Posey's and Gibson's. Whereas Posey and Gibson stress Indian dialect and history or other Indian-related issues as a way to create as sympathetically as possible the specific political and social context for Indianness, Eddleman Reed tries to eliminate "Indianness" from her magazine; instead, she uses *Twin Territories* as a means to bridge boundaries that separate "whites" from "Indians," emphasizing Indians who are well-educated and accomplished individuals. She candidly explains her motivation for running her column:

> So much is being written and reported to the great daily and weekly newspapers published in the northern and eastern states concerning Indian Territory which is absolutely false and misleading that *Twin Territories* deems it an imperative duty resting

upon the editors of papers and periodicals published in Indian
Territory to contradict and denounce all such fabrications. (152)

Like Gibson and Posey, but in a dramatically different manner, Eddleman
Reed "rewrites" Indians into her magazine. She responds to many letters
from curious people inquiring about Indians or wanting to know some-
thing about Indian Territory, realizing that a large segment of society is
ignorant or naïve in its knowledge about these topics. Eddleman Reed
attacks the more overt misconceptions about Indian Territory and its peo-
ples in her answer to a letter written by a "Milliner" in Oakhill, New York,
which appeared in January 1902:

> You ask what kind of a stock of millinery you should select to set-
> tle in a town in Indian Territory; also you add, if lots of beads and
> such things are required as trimmings, and if it is true that the
> Indians like only the brightest of colors of ribbon? Really, I ought
> not to pay attention to your questions. What do you take us for?
> Where have you been the last half century? Seriously, I wouldn't
> advise you to come here with a stock of millinery. You're needed
> in that place, I am sure, where you won't be misunderstood—and
> unappreciated. . . . It would be a pity to have you sacrifice your-
> self to come way out here in order to educate them in wearing
> up-to-date-hats. . . . It wouldn't pay you my dear madam—but
> you might learn a whole lot! (153)

Eddleman Reed encounters easterners who not only think bright shiny
objects entice Indians but who also believe that they eat insects. "None
of the Indians in Indian Territory, nor anywhere else," she writes back
to "Edith," a resident of Merrill, Wisconsin, "that I know of eat bugs
and grasshoppers. What do you take us for out here?" (*Twin Territories,*
February 1901). Eddleman Reed subtly demonstrates her wide array of
knowledge as she directs her reader to a specific issue of *Scientific American*
that features "dainty dishes" that Filipino people eat. Eddleman Reed tells
her reader that she must have superimposed Indians on these more exotic
aboriginal people.

Eddleman Reed's sometimes flippant responses demonstrate her
aggravation in dealing with people who think of Indians as the "uncivi-
lized other." But as her response to the reader's letter reveals, Eddleman
Reed, like Posey, often takes a humorous bent in her editorials. She mis-
chievously turns a paranoid man over to the mercy of his wife, hinting that

he should fear the sting of her whip more than the "wild" Indians. This question to the editor reflects easterners' ignorance about the territory:

> J. A. K. Westfield Mass (a) It is no more dangerous to live in Indian Territory than any part of the United States (b) Yes, you are safe in bringing your wife with you—so far as I know. I am not acquainted with her, but if she doesn't whip you, no one here will, so long a you are a law-abiding citizen. (Morrison, 153–54)

Another person, B.A.R. from Galesville, Wisconsin, inquires about the whereabouts of a man whom he fears may have been killed by "wild" Indians. Eddleman Reed corrects his misconceptions about Indian Territory and playfully volunteers to help him look for "clues" in his Wild West fantasy about his missing friend. Eddleman Reed writes: "I don't think your suggestion that he may have been killed by wild Indians is a correct one, for there are no wild Indians here. Write again. You may find him yet, and if I obtain any clues, I shall take pleasure in letting you know" (*Twin Territories*, April 1901).

Perhaps in an effort to erase the "wild" Indian picture that many easterners held about Indian Territory, Eddleman Reed redesigned the cover of *Twin Territories*, which featured two Plains Indians galloping on horseback. Beneath the picture, a bold black subtitle proclaimed: "Twin Territories, The Indian Magazine, published for the Indians of Indian Territory and Oklahoma." The new cover highlighted a bare-chested Indian in full headdress, buckskins, and moccasins, standing next to a "new" Indian garbed in trousers and a jacket, evidently wearing the attire of a "civilized Indian."[8] The background shows factories along with tipis, indicating the "signs" of a new era.

Eddleman Reed worked arduously to refashion Indian images in her magazine. Along with her editorial column, she ran a feature entitled "Types of Indian Girls," which displayed photos of beautiful and accomplished young Indian women, usually wearing fashionable dresses. For example, the January 1903 issue highlights Mrs. Florence Stephens-Lennon. Wearing a sleeveless black dress, she gazes into a book that she holds in her lap. The caption under her photo emphasizes her accomplishments: "A beautiful Cherokee woman. One of the most accomplished musicians of Indian Territory." Mrs. Czarina Colbert Conlan is also featured in the same issue; wearing a lacy, white, high-necked dress, she looks off the page. Her caption reads: "Prominent in Indian Territory Club

Circles. First Vice President of the Indian Territory and Oklahoma Territory Federation of Clubs. Mrs. Conlan will edit new Club Department in Twin Territory."

Eddleman Reed displays Indian women who defy the popular misconception of the Indian "squaw" held by so many of her eastern subscribers. In most of the Indian women photos, readers must look for "traces" of Indianness, for these women epitomize strong and influential society women most often thought of as Euroamerican. Eddleman Reed informs us about Indian women's various accomplishments, collapsing derogatory images that her eastern readers may harbor about these "Native" women. Her obvious intention is to link these women with Euroamerican women who were "cultured," educated, and active members of various social and charitable clubs. Eddleman Reed counters invisibility with visibility; she fights erasure by ardently defending her position that "there is nothing improper or bold in a young lady allowing her picture to appear in her magazine," stating that she wants "to show the world that the Territory people are up-to-date" (Morrison, 152). Whereas Posey and Gibson use este charte and strong Indian figures to achieve power, Eddleman Reed chose to mask her Indian women figures, making them appear like white women. Her images, of course, appealed to her Euroamerican audience.

Eddleman Reed, Gibson, and Posey gradually achieved literary prominence; but for the most part, mainstream culture at large still envisioned Indians as "wild" or "uncivilized." These Indian writers were being absorbed into a Euroamerican narrative that continued to deny Indians proper representation. They fought back in a public forum, influencing both easterners and Indians, refashioning and rewriting their own Indian narratives and their own ways of envisioning Indianness.

One of their contributions was their attempt to shatter old Indian images and establish new images, forcing mainstream culture not to exclude them. Gibson's "Rifle Shots" provided a forum for less-conservative Creeks as he vented his anger and frustration about the failure of the federal government in dealing with his fellow Creeks. Using a different strategy, Posey, through his Fus Fixico characters, also commented on the current political situation in Indian Territory, while Eddleman Reed refashioned visual images of Indian women in *Twin Territories*.

In order to write themselves into history, all three authors recognized the importance of bonding together. Gibson and Posey spoke to one another in their individual columns, encouraging their audience to read one another's editorials. Eddleman Reed also published short stories, poems, and biographical information about Gibson and Posey in her magazine, and Posey promoted Eddleman Reed's magazine in the *Indian Journal.* Counteracting invisibility hinged upon bringing forth multiple Indian voices. Cooperation and putting aside political differences became important in order to withstand erasure. As Gibson notes at the time of Posey's death, "He had worked for the best for his people, and always extended the right hand of fellowship" (*Indian Journal,* June 5, 1908). These writers circle around each other, perhaps ironically, forming a strong and meaningful literary bond while acknowledging each other's work, commenting upon it, and assisting each other to become visible to a local audience and, later, to a national one.

3

CIRCUMVENTING SPEECH
WESTERN POETICS AND THE SHAPING OF INDIAN TERRITORIES

*The Indian talks in poetry; poetry is his vernacular—not neces-
sarily the stilted poetry of books, but the free and untrammeled
poetry of Nature, the poetry of the fields, the sky, the river, the sun
and stars. In his own tongue it is not difficult for the Indian to
compose,—he does it instinctively.*
                                                    —*Alex Posey*[1]

Posey wrote poems about eminent Indian Territory leaders such as Crazy
Snake and Sequoyah, as well as about ordinary Indians like Hotgun and
Yadeka Harjo, and about Creek ball game festivities. Like Thoreau, Posey
was inspired by the natural landscape; images from the surrounding coun-
tryside of his home in Indian Territory appear in his various nature poems.
Posey was influenced by and admired Thoreau and, like him, often perceived
the Indian romantically, as "one with nature" and, lamentably, as a van-
ishing breed. Posey thus views Indians as if he were a Euroamerican. On
the other hand, Posey wanted to keep alive his Indian heritage, and he
wrote about Creek verbal traditions and the Indian's ability to outlast the
Euroamerican. Posey's Euroamerican education and his Indian roots often
seem to create conflict for him as a Creek writer. In his poetry, Posey strug-
gles with his heritage, sometimes celebrating his Indian identity, at other
times distancing himself from his culture, in an effort to find his poetic voice.

Living approximately fifty years after Thoreau, Posey parallels Thoreau's
mystical and reverent regard for nature. Posey himself is quick to note the
resemblance to Thoreau. He writes in a letter to acquaintance Fred Bard,
correspondent for the *Kansas City Star:* "Thoreau was a man after my own
heart, because, perhaps, there is so much Indian in him. I carry a pocket
edition of *Walden* in my jeans constantly, mainly just to have it near me"
(Marable and Boylan, 79). Situating Thoreau in his place and time and
examining his reverence for nature as well as his ambivalence about the
values of Indian, as compared to Euroamerican, culture will enable the

reader to understand the complicated position of Posey and his poetry; for Posey not only read Thoreau but imitated his journal notes.

Thoreau's life-long recordings of Indian cultures are attempts to situate himself within the American landscape as a means to achieve some understanding of self. He recognizes the Indians' "oneness" with nature. In March 1842, Thoreau records in his journal that as he walks the fields of Concord he is traversing where Native Americans once walked:

> Where ever I go, I tread in the tracks of the Indians. I pick up the bolt which he has but just dropped at my feet. And if I consider destiny I am on his trail. I scatter his hearthstones with my feet, and pick out of the embers of his fire the simple but enduring implements of the wigwam and the chase. In planting my corn in the same furrow which yielded its increase to his support so long, I displace some memorial of him. (*Journal,* 1:337)

Thoreau records Indian cultures in order to understand the self. As he scatters the hearthstones, he scatters the very heart, the home, of the Indian to displace him ultimately. Yet unlike that of the Indians whom he meticulously studies, Thoreau's destiny is that of the Euroamerican, and he is bound to displace the Indians. Thoreau's own excursions into the Maine woods and his sojourn at Walden Pond are efforts to achieve a renewed, transcendent self. But his jaunts into the woods did not deter him from accepting the Euroamerican idea of progress. Thoreau's cabin at Walden Pond, after all, was just a short jump from the railroad tracks.

Posey avidly read Thoreau's prolific journal writings and *Walden,* from which he imbibes Thoreau's view of nature and his particular way of writing about it. Posey imitates Thoreau by writing his own field notes, recording details about various trees, birds, flowers, and other wildlife. One early spring day, for example, Posey observes an abundance of wood violets; on another day he writes that the wind changed direction, blowing north and harder than any other day; he also makes note of a black-capped chickadee, a cardinal, and a mockingbird, the new foliage of several fruit trees, and a full-fledged "war" between a black wasp and a leaf worm ("Notes Afield").

Many of Posey's poems render the beauty and minute details of his Oklahoman landscape. In "Bob White," for instance, he tries to recreate the feeling of the bobwhite, whose song permeates the air with its gentle sound and represents poetically the feeling of the quiet of the woods. In the second stanza, Posey captures the bobwhite's song, cutting through the silence, reverberating through the woods:

> And when the cheery voice is dead,
> And silence woos the wind to rest
> Among the oak boughs overhead,
> From valley, hill, or meadow's breast,
> There comes an answ'ring call—
> Bob-Bob White!

> (lines 7–12)

In the third stanza, Posey notes the undulation of the waning evening light shining down on the earth, as "light and shadow play / At hide-and-seek behind the high / Blue walls around the day" (lines 14–17). The final stanza ends in the whirling, frantic flight of the bobwhite as it "whirreth, like a missile shot, into a neigh / b'ring tree" (lines 20–21). The bird's departure startles the speaker; this interruption is reminiscent of the train's whistle that pierced the quiet of Walden Pond during Thoreau's deep contemplation. Thoreau informs his readers that "the whistle of the locomotive penetrates my woods summer and winter, sounding like the scream of a hawk sailing over some farmers' yard" (*Walden*, 131). Of course, Thoreau's disruption leads to his long harangue about the inevitable displacement of his forest solitude by civilization. While the poem "Bob White" leaves the reader lingering at the edge of twilight as it pulls the speaker deeper into the dark mysteries of nature, Thoreau becomes shaken from the natural beauty that surrounds him when he hears the train's whistle.

In "Bob White" the bird plays with the presence and absence of sound, shadow and light, and animate and inanimate objects. Its poignancy comes from the moment at twilight when a burst of melodious song resounds from a solitary bird, followed by the absolute quiet of the evening. The speaker informs the reader about the bird: "a speck of brown adown" fades into the evening twilight, flitting "where the wood and prairie meet, / Across the tasseled corn and waving wheat" (lines 18–23). However, as the bobwhite disappears, so does the "sound" the bobwhite makes, as heard by English speakers. Posey may be at home in the meadows and prairies, but he chooses English to express his poetic feelings.

Whereas "Bob White" focuses on the "English" sound that a bird in flight makes, the poem "To the Crow" tries to capture the eeriness, the stark loneliness, that one feels when listening to a raucous crow. In contrast to "Bob White," "To the Crow" is simple and direct:

Caw, caw, caw.
Thou bird of ebon hue,
Above the slumb'rous valley spread in flight,
On wings that flash defiance back at light,
A speck against the blue,
A-vanishing.

(lines 1–6)

Yet as in "Bob White," the speaker in "To the Crow" hints at his inability to affix or discern nature. In the second stanza, the speaker suggests his incompetency in "reading" nature:

Thou bird of common sense,
Far, far in lonely distance leaving me,
Deluded, with a shout of mockery
For all my diligence
At evening

(lines 8–12)

In this particular poem nature appears impenetrable to, somehow ungraspable by, the speaker.

Like Posey, Thoreau professed an interest in birds and other wildlife. He felt compelled, in March 1845, to move to a secluded place where he could devote his time to writing and to studying the natural environment. Cutting down pine trees with a borrowed ax on the north shore of Walden Pond, Thoreau eventually moved into his small cabin and commenced writing *Walden*.

Thoreau, satisfied in his new home, experienced such a sense of harmony with his surroundings that he could barely find the words to express himself. He writes in *Walden:* "Sympathy with the fluttering alder and popular leaves almost takes my breath" (146). Enjoying nature, he asks: why should people wish to be living adjacent to the depot, the post office, the barroom, the meeting house, the school house, or the grocery? (150). Thoreau maintained the belief that he had found companionship with the "sweet and tender" society of nature.

Similarly, "When Molly Blows the Dinnerhorn," perhaps drawing on Posey's memories of childhood, illustrates a fondness for country living;

this poem conjures up the smells and activities associated with "down-home" cooking.[2]

> The cabbage steams, and bacon's fat;
> The bread is made of last year's corn—
> When Molly blows the dinner-horn.
>
> (lines 1–4)

In the third stanza, the poet describes the smoke curling up from a cabin's chimney, conveying the feeling of ease and enjoyment of rustic life; even the old dog, sprawled on the kitchen floor, is content:

> The cur, erstwhile stretched in a snore,
> Lays stout siege to the kitchen door;
> Nor will he raise it, or be gone,
> When Molly blows the dinner-horn.
>
> (lines 13–16)

Posey depicts what seems to be the easy country living of rural Oklahoma in this poem. Posey's "The Call of the Wild" also echoes Thoreau's desire to free himself from society. The poem focuses on the speaker's inability to be confined within the four walls of a house and on his longing for the freedom of living under the open sky. Just as Thoreau felt cleansed by his interaction with nature, one of the prevalent ideas in "The Call of the Wild" is that nature not only tugs at the heart but also "purifies" the speaker:

> I'm tired of the gloom
> In a four-walled room;
> Hearty-weary, I sigh
> For the open sky,
> And the solitude
> Of the greening wood;
> Where the bluebirds call,
> And the sunbeams fall,
> And the daisies lure
> The soul to be pure.[3]
>
> (lines 1–10)

The second stanza describes nature as a river that sings the "murmur of the rills / In the breezy hills" (lines 15–16), beckoning the speaker to give

up the "ways of strife." Posey incorporates various conventions of roman-
ticism when he evokes the image of Pan:

> the pipe of Pan—
> The hairy half-man—
> The bright silence breaks
> By the sleeping lakes
>
> (lines 17–20)

Posey is not, then, the "simple" Indian of Thoreau's imagination or expe-
riences, but an educated man, just as much at home in the woods as in the
world of Greek mythology. In the above poem, quite clearly, Posey under-
stands the "call" of nature. It is evident that the landscape pulls at the
poet's heart, and he uses romantic tropes to convey images that are just as
natural for him as images of his Tulledega Hills.

Indeed, according to poet George Riley Hall, one of Posey's friends,
when both men visited the Tulledega Hills, Posey's poetic voice soared.
Hall said that here Posey "was in tune with the beautiful in nature. It
thrilled him" (Littlefield, *Posey,* 107). Hall further states that Posey "loved
the shining reaches of Limbo Creek that winds it way through the
Tulledega Hills, but above all he loved to lie under the whispering pines
of the mountains and listen, in rapt silence, to the crooning melody of the
forest. They touched his poet-soul with the magic of the wild, and lingered
in his memory forever" (107).

Both Posey and Thoreau possessed a thoroughly romantic belief about
the coexistence of Indians with nature and their ability to express thoughts
and ideas more poetically than Europeans. And both Posey and Thoreau
felt that Indians were more receptive to the mysteries and revelations of
nature. Thoreau writes in his journal:

> The charm of the Indian to me is that he stands free and uncon-
> strained in Nature, is her inhabitant and not her guest, and wears
> her easily and gracefully. But the civilized man has the habits of
> the house. His house is a prison, in which he finds himself
> oppressed and confined, not sheltered and protected. (*Journal,*
> 1:253)

Posey's desire to be severed from the cumbersome life of "civilized"
living is quite evident in "Tulledega," where his childhood memories
remain as a "symbol of remoteness and natural beauty" (Littlefield, *Posey,* 23):

Hedged in, shut up with low log cabins built—
How snugly!—in the quaint old fashioned way;
With fields of yellow maize, so small that you
Might hide them with your palm while gazing on
Them from the hills around them, high and blue.
Hedged in, shut up with long forgotten ways.

(lines 7–12)

Even though "Tulledega" reaffirms Posey's love of nature, we should exam-
ine this poem a little more closely. "Tulledega" is one of the few poems in
which Posey reiterates a phrase—"Hedged in, shut up"—and it is a refrain
that haunts the speaker, setting the tone for the entire poem. Although the
poem can be read as a simple declaration of nostalgia for Posey's child-
hood landscape, his repetition of this refrain imparts an important sym-
bolic significance to the meaning of the poem:

Hedged in, shut up with long forgotten ways,
And stories handed down from Sire to son.
Hedged in, shut up with broad Oktaha, like
A flash of glory curled among the hills.

(lines 12–15)

The poem alludes to the poet's struggle to fit in two worlds and express the
difficulty he experiences in a world that does not wholeheartedly embrace
cultural differences. The poem is central to the author's own position as an
Indian poet trying to express himself. The reiteration of the refrain "Hedged
in, shut up" connotes the sense that the speaker is unable to transmit the
stories "handed down from Sire to son." The speaker states that the stories
are hidden away, "shut up with broad Oktaha." It is possible that Posey him-
self, as his persona in "Tulledega," suffers an identity crisis when he real-
izes that he cannot recover his own Creek verbal tradition:

Hedged in, shut up and hidden from the world,
As though it said, "I have no words for you;
I'm not a part of you: your ways aren't mine."

(lines 4–6)

Whereas "The Call of the Wild" reveals Posey's Euroamerican poetic ten-
dencies, "Tulledega" implies something different. Posey's "Europeanized"
side here is alien; he desires to get back to "himself, the Indian"—or at

least the speaker feels "hedged in, shut up and hidden from the world." The landscape and Oktaha's stories appear inaccessible to the poet; he has lost any sense of "oneness" with nature and with traditional Creek culture. The words "I have no words for you" hint at the possibility that there are no words for Posey either, who has, on the surface at least, cast his lot with the Euroamerican world. Posey may speak Creek, but he feels inarticulate and silenced. "Tulledega" reveals possible fissures in Posey's thinking that allow his readers access into his intricate and complicated world.

Thoreau likewise desired to experience the indescribable power of nature. For Thoreau, no other people so effectively integrated themselves with the natural environment as Indians. He looks to them as representative of natural people, as human beings emanating from nature. Again and again, this idea appears in Thoreau's writing. Because of his fascination with Indians and his love of the wilderness, Thoreau was compelled to return to Maine two more times, in 1853 and 1857, when he would learn as much as he could about the Indian lifestyle by hunting, fishing, and traveling via canoe with his Indian guides, Joe Polis and Joe Aitteon. Like Posey, Thoreau experiences nature firsthand as he rambles along the shore of a lake at midnight:

> The little rill tinkles the louder, and peoples all the wilderness for me; and the glassy smoothness of the sleeping lake, lapping the shores of the new world, with the dark, fantastic rocks rising here and there from its surface, made a scene not easily described. It has left such an impression of stern, yet gentle, wildness on my memory as will not be effaced. (*Maine Woods*, 40)

By experiencing nature in the "raw," Thoreau obtained firsthand knowledge about Indians' coexistence with nature. There is one moment in *The Maine Woods* when Thoreau actually does come to terms with Indians' lifestyle and appears very comfortable with his Indian guides. He writes that one evening he sat by the campfire, listening to the "purely wild and primitive American sound" of the Indians' language (Sayre, 171). The Indians tell him a good story about a deer running loose through Bangor, or as the Indian humorously calls it, "the deer that went a shopping."[4] Thoreau seems to be on good terms with his Indian companions and shows interest in their experiences as he asks them about specific Indian place names. Later that same evening Thoreau boasts, "I stood, or rather lay, as near to primitive man of America, that night, as any of its discoverers ever did" (*Maine Woods,* 137).

For Thoreau, Indians represent pristine nature. Indians become as nature and merge with it:

> The pine stands in the woods like an Indian,—untamed, with a fantastic wildness about it, even in the clearings. If an Indian warrior were well painted, with pines in the background, he would seem to blend with the trees, and make a harmonious expression. The pitch pines are the ghosts of Philip and Massasoit. The white pine has the smoother features of the squaw. (*Journal,* 1:258)

Thoreau's imaginative re-creation of the Indian as symbolic of nature's pristine state is an attempt to reinvent the primal world. There is some evidence that Thoreau desired, as Fussell states, to supply his fellow Americans with an image of the Indian as "more primitive, more mythical, more shadowy and unreal than anything the upstarty Europeans could boast" (332). The shadowy, mythical Indian captures Thoreau's imagination. He writes in his journal: "Lo, the poor Indian! . . . There is always a slight haze or mist on the brow of the Indian" (*Journal,* 10:77).

Thoreau looks to Indians as the key to a mythical people whose basic nature has not yet been corrupted by civilization. Though Thoreau admired Indians, believing they represented a state not really obtainable, he also upheld an equally narrow view of Indians as degenerates. This paradoxical position becomes evident in *The Maine Woods* when he describes "a short shabby washer-woman-looking Indian" that lands "his" canoe near a grocery store and carries a bundle of skins in one hand and "an empty keg or half-barrel in the other, and scrambles up the bank" (6). Thoreau's obvious inference reflects what many Euroamericans believed—that alcoholism and degeneracy would destroy Indian cultures. In spite of maintaining romantic beliefs about Indians, Thoreau believed that Indians would be destroyed by their excessive drinking. For as Thoreau fixes his gaze on the raggedy "washer-woman" Indian with the keg of rum nestled securely under his arm, he remarks that "this picture will do to put before the Indian's history, that is, the history of extinction" (6). Thus Indians embody a number of conflicting images: they could represent cultural erosion or primitively pure human beings, or they could symbolize an image of the present, "the spirit of the past entering and animating the heavy body of the contemporary" (Fussell, 337).

On the one hand Thoreau invents Indians who are purely fabrications of his imagination, the "romantic" and supposedly exalted others whom he desires. On the other hand, he constructs an image that relegates them to being inferior to Euroamericans. Thoreau's inventions of Indians demonstrate his inability to reconcile these contradictory images. Posey, like Thoreau, also constructs a similar image of Indians. In "Tulledega," Posey is trying to capture what eludes him. Even though Posey appears to be Europeanized, writing of Pan and so on, he also desires to get back to nature, to find his Indian roots. Ironically, by using Thoreau's Europeanized example, Posey searches for his Indian identity. At times he does take on the mythologizing tendencies of Thoreau; however, he presents another dimension of Indians that situates him apart from Thoreau.

Posey illustrates his paradoxical position when he writes his long epic poem, "The Indian's Past Olympic," a description of a Creek ball game. Like Thoreau, who desires to reinvent a mythical world inhabited by Indians, Posey tries to capture and mythologize a time, perhaps even before the European invasion, when the Creeks enacted the pomp and pageantry of the ball game. It is evident that Posey looks to his Creek verbal tradition as a means to recover his Indian heritage. Yet even though Posey's poem is sentimental and a romanticized picture of this event, he gives a fairly accurate account of the Creek ball game and its ensuing activities.[5] This poem is not like Thoreau's attempt to merge the Indian with the trees. Rather, that Posey calls the ball game an "Olympic" reveals his attempt to merge the Indians' game with earlier Greek heroic games. Moreover, he uses the epic heroic form of the most "advanced" civilization the West has known, especially at his time. Ironically, Thoreau maintains an anticivilization stance, while Posey romanticizes and mythologizes Indian cultures, placing them at the "beginning" of civilization. However, his linking these games to Creek verbal traditions demonstrates his desire to construct an image that most Euroamericans might desire to have about Indians.

The ball game, played by the Creeks, Choctaws, Chickasaws, Seminoles, and Cherokees, with slight variations, appears to have had religious significance, besides being a popular social event. The object of the game was to put a small ball, usually made of hair and covered with deerskin (Swanton, *Indians,* 675), between two poles, which were connected with a cross pole near the top (D. Green, 14). The ball was carried by small lacrosse-like rackets constructed of curved sticks. Usually, teams from towns or clans would compete against each other (Wright, 37; Swanton,

Indians, 677). The game was large, with as many as nine to twelve players on each side, but some records indicate that there were sometimes up to fifty players on one side (Swanton, *Indians,* 675). Apparently, the most popular time for hosting a ball game was in the fall, after the corn had been harvested, because the people had more time for such activities then (Mooney, "Cherokee," 110).

In order to feed the numerous participants in and spectators of the ball game, as "The Indian's Past Olympic" suggests, much food was prepared before the game. The poem also alludes to religious taboos that the ball players were required to follow:

> In mounds high heaps the rip'ning corn,
> Which warriors dare not touch, disdain
> Till now, and bisons from the plain,
> Wild turkeys, bears and antelopes
> From shady wilds and mountain slopes,
> And meats from all the woods around,
> Doth grace the ancient, sacred ground,
> Where painted nations group in one
> To shout the praise of battles won.
>   (lines 2–10)

After the players and spectators gather and take their respective places, according to one observer, the game opens with a long oration by an elder chief who recalled past ball games; the oration, reportedly delivered with much exuberance, was intended to rouse the players and to inspire them to play well (Swanton, *Indians,* 676). Other accounts of the ball game mention the mixing and distribution of the "black drink," which is brewed by boiling caseena leaves,[6] which give it a dark color. The concoction is put into a conch shell and distributed among the male members of the tribe. The drinking of the black drink is accompanied by long "yahola" cries— a deep yell accompanied by a shrill yell, which is held as long as possible (Wright, 26; Swanton, *Indians,* 764). The black drink is associated with purification, peace, and sociability (Wright, 26):

> The prophet, plumed, slow taps the drum,
> Exclaims aloud: "Old Warriors come
> And drink this noble drink I give,
> And thus prolong the years you live,

As did your fathers, slumb'ring sound
Beneath the soil—their native ground.
Cleanse well your souls of former sin
And all the vile that lurks within;
Begin anew as doth the year
And young you'll be when death is near."
(lines 15–24)

The players, garbed in breechcloth, painted, and greased with the chewed bark of either an elm or a sassafras, are arranged on the ball field (Mooney, "Cherokee," 124). Finally the game begins.

The ball is tossed, thro' air serene,
With speed, it flies on wings unseen.
With ball-sticks pointing to the skies
Each warrior stands with watchful eyes;
And like a thunderbolt that's hurled
From heaven downward to the world,
Hard strikes the ball upon the ground,
And gives the ear its muffled sound.
The warriors whoop and whooping bound
As lions on the shepherd's pen,
Loud blends the shouts of savage men.
(lines 27–37)

The poem then recounts the viciousness of the players as they try to score points for their own team; the poem, with gruesome detail, describes the wounds and injuries of the players:

High to and fro the ball is thrown,
And gaping wounds by war clubs torn,
Gush torrents, streams of clotting gore.
(lines 40–43)

Along with depicting the game, the poem describes the cleansing of the players and the feast and festivities that occur after the game:

And now a pool each warrior seeks
And bathes his gory form and scars
Beneath the gleaming twilight stars.
Lo! gorgeous heaps of flesh are spread,

And piles of most delicious bread
Which scent the straying zephyrs round:
Each warrior's seated on the ground,
And smiling maids their wants supply.
                    (lines 67–74)

Next, the poem focuses on the more "exotic" and "primitive" elements of the event. With the moon up, giving the night an eerie ambiance, the prophet shakes his gourd to the rhythm of some ancient dance; while lifting high his jeweled hand, he instructs the dancers to "Heap the flame— / As burns the blaze so burns our fame!" (lines 100–101). The tone of the poem shifts as the Indians become more demonlike:

And fiery sparks, like met'ors, rush
High upward thro' the woods and brush,
Revealing all the savage host,
Of life regardless, and its cost;
Eyes like burnished em'ralds gleaming—
Strange in form—as demons seeming.
                    (lines 102–7)

One can almost imagine the dancers stepping to the tempo of the bass drums, while the prophet chants "their battle-lays." The dancers' "war-whoop's loud alarms" echo into the dark night; finally, the sky slowly changes color, becoming tinged with gray.

The luna-orb has lost its way.
Day blossoms crimson in the east
And ends the dance, the play and feast.
                    (lines 133–36)

The poem shifts from elevating Indians, describing the Indians' "Golden Age," a time of copious foods, merriment, and wise prophets, and turns in another direction, creating utter distance from the speaker by emphasizing the primitivism of the Indian participants as they play a bloody and strenuous ball game. Even though Posey's depiction of the violence of the game does not seem to be exaggerated, the poem changes focus from stressing the Indians' idyllic communal state to commenting on what the speaker believes are the Indians' uncivilized beliefs and morals.

Like Thoreau, who kept Indians, for the most part, at a mythical distance while celebrating their simplistic lifestyle, Posey gives us the idyllic harvest, the sacred grounds, and the gaping wounds of the warriors. He describes how the Creek players mangle and kill each other on the field:

> In mis'ry, pain, remorse untold
> Lies groaning, foiled the warrior bold—
> Unquenched his thirst, unkissed his lips,
> Unmourned his fate—death angel grips
> The valiant form, the lifeless brave
> And wings him, sleeping, to his grave;
> Uncoffined there and left alone,
> To dust returning, bone by bone.
> And not one drop of tear is shed,
> Or words of grief or sorrows said
> By those who watch or those who play,
> Where men their kindreds, fellows slay.
> (lines 48–59)

Still, the warrior is bold, valiant, even though he is "demonlike." Unlike Thoreau's romanticized Indians, Posey shows us more complex Indians precisely because the picture of the Creek ball game is so rich and diverse. "The Indian's Past Olympic" describes an idyllic time long ago, but juxtaposes other details of Indian ritual and practices. Moreover, the poem presents the traditions and rituals of the past. Even though Posey's tendency is to romanticize the event, he does capture the multilayered activities of the ritual with its "frenzied" dance, play, rest, and feast. Along with its ritualistic content, the poem focuses on this "frenzied" dancing, alluding to the Indians' demonlike behavior. The poet also points out the players' apparent indifference to death. Posey differs greatly from Thoreau, who chose to write about romantic Indian activities. In *The Maine Woods*, for instance, he describes the "beautiful simplicity" of a singing Indian, whom he encounters on his journey (179). Thoreau thinks of Indians in a positive, idyllic way; his Indians are of nature. To be sure, they are "distanced" and something even of his invention; on the other hand, Posey depicts a more realistic picture of Indian life. Posey's warriors are tangible; Thoreau's "mystical" Indians slip along the rivers.

Not only does Posey describe the warriors' bravery as they play arduously, but he stresses their custom of leaving injured players to suffer on the ball field, practices that do not fit Thoreau's notion of romanticized Indians. Why does Posey choose to include such conflicting and uncomplimentary elements in his epic poem, elements that seem to undermine his purpose of extolling his Creek ancestors? Yet Posey does not appear aware that his views about his Creek ancestors are conflicted. He instead seems to believe that his ancestors were simple and childlike. Or he simply may wish to maintain distance from these Indians, to keep them within the "mythical mist."

Posey juxtaposes two possibilities of viewing Indians, with no attempt to reconcile incongruent images, believing them already reconciled. He does not seem able to extricate himself from the inconsistencies in which he finds himself. After all, he may not have been able to "control" or "manage" the contradictions; the gaps between one view of the Indian, the valiant warrior, and another, the savage demon-player, are not glossed over. Even though the contradictions seem glaring to us, it is unclear how Posey or even his readers at that time may have viewed these seeming disjunctions.

Vacillating between two world perspectives is not unique to Posey; many other early Native American writers, like Charles Eastman, a Santee Sioux who earned a medical degree and wrote several autobiographical works, including *Indian Boyhood* (1902) and *From the Deep Woods* (1916), illustrate the difficulties in positioning one's self between two worlds.[7] But Posey's "The Indian's Past Olympic" suspends two views of Indians. In other words, as in the "idyllic" or "valiant" warrior, the poem stresses the innocence and simple ways of Indian life as being somewhat admirable but also focuses on Indian cruelties and assigns them negative attributes. Because he equally privileges the more positive images of Indians with contradictory ones, Posey's portrayal of American Indians ultimately leads to the inevitable question: who is Posey's American Indian?

As we examine Posey's poetry, it becomes evident that he tries to maintain a delicate balance. He shows a fascination with the dichotomous stereotype of the Indian: the images of the savage and the degenerate. Along with these predominant images of Indians emerge what Dippie calls the "rhetoric of doom"; the Indian with all his manifestations was perceived as being at the "sunset of his existence" (13). Or as Eliza Lee wrote about Indians in 1847, "One by one they perish, like the leaves of the forest that are swept away by the autumn winds; melancholy shrouds them; they die of sadness, are effaced from the earth by an inexorable destiny" (Dippie, 13). According to both Euroamericans and Native Americans, it was inevitable that Indians would disappear or would be assimilated into mainstream society—either way, they would no longer be an obstacle to

Euroamerican expansion. Posey's "An Outcast" mirrors this belief, stressing the speaker's inevitable death:

> By winds that chase with lifted spear,
> A leaf, blood-stained, fell spent at last
> Pursued across the waning year,
> Upon my bosom, poor Outcast!
>   (lines 1–4)

Posey's poetic sensibilities intuit the position that he maintains; his ambivalence, or rather his vacillation between conflicting images, uncovers his own difficulty in negotiating two divergent views of Indians. "An Outcast" obliquely alludes to the tension surrounding these differences.

The poem's imagery alludes to fall, when leaves turn red as they die. Posey chooses not to "subvert" *leaf* and *blood-stained* but places them alongside each other. The image "blood-stained" is striking, but fitting. "Blood-stained" links the dying year to the "dying" Indian culture, so that "leaf," "outcast," and "blood-stained" are not merely representative of cultural differences but signify death. The Indians are like the old year: they too will wane and fall, becoming blood-stained outcasts. These lines appear prophetic and poignant.

To a degree, Posey does succumb to contemporary thinking by believing that Indians should embrace dominant society. Following the lead of some eminent mainstream thinkers, most notably Thoreau, Posey also laments the passing of Indians. His poem "Hotgun on the Death of Yadeka Harjo" parallels the idea of the solitary Vanishing Indian; however, Posey also reveals a contrary stance by satirizing the concept of the Vanishing Indian through his character Hotgun, who "persists":

> "Well so," Hotgun he say,
> "My ol' time frien', Yadeka Harjo, he
> Was died the other day,
> An' they was no ol' timer left but me.
>   (lines 1–4)

In this poem, more than any other, Posey cuts loose from convention, from flattened, two-dimensional Indian stereotypes, and shows an old Indian man, Hotgun, chatting with his friend, Wolf Warrior, who listens "close" to Hotgun's words, along with Kono Harjo, who also "pay close 'tention too." The men gather to hear Hotgun tell the local gossip. Hotgun laments the change in times as he says, "Hotulk Emathla he / Was go to be good Injin long time 'go" (lines 6–8). Hotgun reminisces about the good old days, noting that even Woxie Harjoche "Been dead ten years or twenty, maybe so." Posey implies that these "old Indians" are the last of a kind, but he does not take the melancholic or tragic stance of his contemporaries. Instead, he chooses an approach that in some ways shows the strength and tenacity of his "Vanishing Indians." Hotgun takes control as he humorously pokes fun at his own inevitable death:

> All had to die at las';
> I live long time, but now my days was few;
> 'Fore long poke-weeds an' grass
> Be growin' all aroun' my grave-house, too.'
>   (lines 9–12)

His friends pause and listen; apparently his words penetrate their thoughts, since Tookpafka Micco "almos' / Let his pipe go out a time or two." Ironically, the poem appears to be about a recently deceased friend, Yadeka Harjo, but really it concerns Hotgun and, by extension, his friends' mortality. Hotgun's tone is lighthearted but serious. He pokes fun at his own grave-house, with weeds and grass strewed around.

The poem illustrates how successfully Posey out-distances much of his other poetry. Instead of the mythical Indians of "The Indian's Past Olympic," this poem speaks "Indian"; he literally uses Indian dialect, which gives the poem credibility and convincingly captures the ideas and philosophies of Hotgun and his friends. The Indians have adapted—they speak a pidgin English, composed of Creek and English words. But they surely do not represent the Thoreauvian "Vanishing Indian." Nevertheless the Indians are, in Thoreau's terms, "civilized," or to some extent Euroized. Posey, however, turns the image inside out, finally severing himself from Thoreau. Indeed, Hotgun exemplifies the tenacity of the Indian to outlast and, perhaps, even out-maneuver Euroamericans.

Posey puts powerful words in Hotgun's mouth, which contrast with the flat, two-dimensional Indian image. Hotgun shows one-upmanship by besting Euroamericans at their own game. Unlike Posey's "The Indian's Past Olympic," "Hotgun on the Death of Yadeka Harjo" renders the strength and the humor of Posey and his Indian ancestors. Posey, sometimes sentimental and whimsical, at other times provocative, but nevertheless with a powerful voice, quite effectively demonstrates the contradictory and paradoxical position of an American Indian poet. On the one hand, his poetry perpetuates Thoreau and other Euroamericans' beliefs and ideas about nature and Indians. On the other hand, many of his poems are careful renderings of his Oklahoma countryside and speak directly and simply about the beauty of nature. In addition, Posey has another important role in American literature. Thoreau ponders in his journal, "What do our anniversaries commemorate but white man's exploits? For the Indian deed there must be an Indian memory; the white man will remember his own only" (*Journal*, 1:443–44). Posey is the Indian voice recreating the splendor of former Creek ball games, rustic life in Indian Territory, and accomplishments of eminent Indian leaders such as Crazy Snake and Sequoyah. His struggle to write poetry about his life and about Indians reflects the difficulties of creating an Indian identity in an era that was undergoing rapid social, political, and economic transformation. Posey's poetry shows a real deftness when he makes use of the oral tradition, of the folklore of his people, or when he transmits "gossip." Hotgun laments, "they was no ol' timer left but me," alluding to his inevitable demise. But his words are contradicted by his voice, articulated through Posey, for the Hotgun poetry reunifies and keeps alive collective Indian memory.

4

REINVENTING TRICKSTER
POSEY'S *NOM DE PLUME,* CHINNUBBIE HARJO

Woetcoh Micco, Waboxie Harjo and Chinnubbie attended Sunday
school at Frozen Rock last Sabbath afternoon. For some reason or
other they did not return when they were expected, and, as a result,
were given one or two demerits. "But," said Waboxie, "what of
that? We recieved [sic] an introduction to the chief's daughter!"
—Chinnubbie[1]

Alex Posey dons the mask of Chinnubbie Harjo, his trickster persona who
frequently finds himself amid embarrassing circumstances or as the hap-
less observer of numerous local events in Indian Territory. While Posey was
attending Bacone Indian University, he also was a reporter for the monthly
B.I.U. Instructor, the school newspaper. Here, as he wrote gossipy news
about school meetings and other activities, Posey gave birth to his persona
Chinnubbie. It was a delivery into an exciting, always ironic, humorous
life in which Chinnubbie continually becomes entangled in awkward
predicaments such as the church meeting with his friends Woetcoh Micco
and Waboxie Harjo, who scoff at the school authorities. Chinnubbie is a
"humorist of unquestioned excellence, as well as being renowned for other
traits of character" ("Chinnubbie and the Owl"). Not only is he a versatile
storyteller, but when he speaks, his listeners are charmed by his eloquence.
Chinnubbie could spin a yarn that "captivated the gravest of his audience."
A truly renowned storyteller, even "his actions when delivering a tale were
as comical and laughable, almost, as the story he told" ("Chinnubbie and
the Owl").

Posey's persona Chinnubbie is derived from his Creek heritage.[2] Posey
attributes his love of Creek tribal stories to the influence of his mother,
Nancy Posey. It is highly probable that she had a good repertoire of sto-
ries about the Creek trickster, Rabbit.[3] Perhaps the deadly and resisting
nature of this trickster appealed to Posey's sensibilities as a writer. Like the
trickster, Posey had a talent for observing the comic side of situations, and

through his detached third-person voice as Chinnubbie Harjo, he entertained his readers with his whimsical and often comic renditions of local happenings (Littlefield, "Evolution," 138).

Through the persona Chinnubbie, Posey wrote humorous comments that appealed to his readers. For example, after mentioning the various students and faculty members who were on the university's sick list, he wrote, "Chinnubbie is not feeling so very well himself" (Littlefield, *Posey,* 55). In another instance, as he describes the local school newspaper picnic, he states that "Chinnubbie sat quietly in the shade, meditating about the weather and the prospects of the farmer" (Littlefield, "Evolution," 138). Like a clever trickster, Chinnubbie shows an uncanny talent for tricking his audience into his chicaneries. In another issue of the Bacone school newspaper, Chinnubbie mentions that the editor had recently received many positive comments about his paper. He adds, "Chinnubbie received a compliment also, but he wisely protests against having it published for he knows he does not deserve it, and even if he did, the step to have it printed would be egotistical."[4] Like Rabbit, who boasts about how much property he owns, Chinnubbie brags about his own editorial skills; trickster-like, he pokes fun at conventions yet successfully outmaneuvers his readers by getting his name mentioned in the newspaper. At an early age, Posey discovered how effective and useful it was to write behind the mask of a trickster figure.

Chinnubbie and the Creek trickster, Rabbit, share the ability to brag or make jokes. Most Creeks would have viewed Chinnubbie as someone whom they knew from their own Rabbit stories, for the Creeks are fond of Rabbit, a wily character who has a tendency to get himself tangled up in ridiculous situations but who, more often than not, still manages to come out relatively unscathed. Perhaps Nancy Posey told Alex one of the numerous stories about Rabbit outwitting and outmaneuvering Wolf. It is probable that tales such as "Rabbit and the Wolf" were told frequently and were part of Posey's childhood experience.

In this tale, Rabbit brags to some girls that he is a big "man" and owns property and a horse. Of course, the girls question Rabbit's truthfulness; he therefore sets out to make a favorable impression on them. Rabbit whines to his friend, Wolf, that he cannot walk to the council meeting and wants to ride there on his back. Wolf, being a good friend, lets Rabbit climb on.

But Rabbit tricks Wolf further by persuading him to let Rabbit put a saddle and then a bridle on Wolf. Finally, Rabbit convinces Wolf that he will feel better wearing his spurs, and he promises not to gouge Wolf's side with them. Before Wolf knows what is going on, Rabbit plunges his steel spurs into his side, then madly gallops by the girls' houses, showing them that he indeed has some "horse" (Swanton, *Myths,* 64).

Some of Rabbit's actions may be conceived as inane or foolish, but other behaviors are viewed as dangerous individualistic expressions that could threaten or undermine existing customs and traditions. Maybe Posey's mother also told him the tale of "How Rabbit Won His Wife's Sister for His Second Wife," which not only shows Rabbit deceiving his wife but pokes fun at existing marriage conventions. The story begins with Rabbit posed romantically: he reclines his head in his wife's lap while she gently massages his head. Rabbit then sees his wife's younger, and more beautiful, sister stroll by. Making some feeble excuse, he runs out of his house and hides in the bushes until his wife's sister passes by. In a disguised voice, he whispers to her that the people have agreed to undertake a big bear hunt, and all the men are to go to a designated camping spot with their wives' sisters, instead of with their own wives.

The young woman runs back to Rabbit's house and tells him and her sister the camp news. She, of course, leaves out the most important part. But with Rabbit's prodding, she reluctantly reveals the information, specifying that each man should leave his wife at home and instead take his wife's sister to the hunt.

Rabbit and his wife make the proper preparations for his departure. When Rabbit and his wife's sister arrive at the arranged camping spot, Rabbit feigns surprise that none of the other hunters has arrived yet. As the sun slowly begins to set, Rabbit tells his wife's sister to make her bed on the other side of the fire, apart from him. Wily Rabbit knows that a big anthill is situated there; his wife's sister tosses and turns all night, scratching at her ant bites. At this crucial moment, Rabbit "began his wooing, and succeeded in winning his second bride" (57).

These trickster tales show that there is no limit to Rabbit's mischievous nature or his vivid imagination. He is clever and creative as he ropes Wolf into acting like a horse or deceives his wife's sister into thinking that he is a kind and caring being. Rabbit demonstrates that he is determined to get what he wants, and in each of these cases, he ends up impressing women. In the first tale, he is clearly the underdog (or should we say underrabbit) as he triumphs over the larger and stronger Wolf. In the second, Rabbit snubs his nose at conventions and gets the "girl," not through his strength, but because he uses his brains. Trickster is a small creature, but he walks tall among his fellow animals: he is able to outwit them and get what he wants, whether from larger animals or even humans.

Trickster portrays a range of cultural possibilities. As he comes up against what every culture envisions as distinct limits, he shows how far these limits can be pushed and, by extension, how far human actions or emotions can go. Trickster treads the line between what is viewed as the sacred and the secular, as his texts both reaffirm and deconstruct societal norms. Yellowman, a Navaho storyteller, tries to pinpoint how this somewhat contradictory figure functions in the Navaho world: "If [Coyote, the Navaho trickster] didn't do all those things, then those things would not be possible in the world" (Wiget, 94).

The trickster is thus a cultural figure who allows Native Americans to envision themselves and their existence. He is a "gut" response to the paradoxical nature of culture: he represents the need to remain within the confines of society and the need to ridicule or reduce societal constraints. Trickster's mask is the mask that Posey dons when he writes about his cultural experience in Indian Territory.

If we look for the site of Posey's trickster-like tendencies, we see that he enjoyed foolish pranks, whether destructive or playful. Both Posey and his father, Lewis Henderson "Hence" Posey, loved a good joke. In June 1897, Posey went to visit his father at his farm near Bald Hill, and he recorded this moment in his journal:

> My father and I scared the renters on the farm into fits with false faces. We run [them] out of the cotton patches and out of their homes and out of their wits. I played the part of the hag and my father that of the devil before day. (Dale, 428)

While playing tricks appealed to Posey's humorous side and seems to have been a favorite pastime, he had another, more scholarly side. Posey was an avid reader, enjoying such subjects as ancient history and biographies of Marcus Antoninus, Marcus Brutus, and Artaxerxes, a Persian king. Posey also was interested in Creek history, and he spent long afternoons chatting about Creek politics and history with Captain Belcher, an old and gregarious gentlemen who was a local history enthusiast.

Posey was also a voracious reader of literature. He read current magazines, including work by popular writers and poets such as Walt Whitman, Washington Irving, and Emily Dickinson. But more than anyone, Robert

Burns appealed to his sensibilities as a writer and poet. Posey describes Burns's impact on him:

I find some new pleasure, some new thought, some new beauty heretofore unseen every time I read poems of the "Ayrshire Plowman." His warm heart, his broad and independent mind "glint" like the daisy in the "histie stubble field" in every song he coraled [*sic*]. (415–16)

Posey's attraction to the "Ayrshire Plowman" parallels his own paradoxical stance. Burns represents a dichotomous self—on the one hand, he is a larger-than-life superScot, a national hero, while on the other hand, he is a man who must struggle, barely surmounting the harsh economic conditions characteristic of his class (McGuirk, 219). Further, Burns took a clear and uncompromising look at himself and compared what he saw to what he thought the Edinburgh gentry desired. From the numerous letters that he wrote to his fellow poets and to some of the established gentry, it becomes apparent that his position was painful. David Sampson points out that Burns was frustrated by a society that denied him entrance because of his lack of aristocratic birth.

It is probable that Posey, who admired Burns's poetry, identified unconsciously with the "Ayrshire Plowman." Like Burns, Posey sought to be accepted in a world that tried to deny him a literary voice. Both Posey and his hero, Burns, understood their positions between two worlds. In several of Burns's verse-epistles, he vacillates between condemning and confirming the gentry's position (Sampson, 35). In spite of his apparent vacillation, Burns's poetry remains political. Burns, estranged from the English gentry, appealed to Posey's sensibilities as a fellow poet, and most likely he was sustained emotionally by this poetry of a person also alienated from mainstream society. Perhaps this is why Posey continually reread and reappreciated Burns's poetry. For like Burns, but in his own manner, Posey makes his writings the site of political ideologies. As he reproduces a strange and powerful commentary about "real" Native peoples living in Indian Territory, he uses language that transgresses the discourse of mainstream American conventions.

Not only does Burns seemed to have influenced Posey, but the Scottish poet's use of dialect appears also to have been important to him. Posey, in order to persuade his friend George Riley Hall, who detested Burns's use of dialect, that the Scotsman was a great poet, recast "To a Mountain

Daisy" in "good English." Posey writes that in "doing so, I fear I have spoiled the poem; for it is in his dialect that Burns is sweetest" (Littlefield, *Posey*, 87). Similarly, Posey's use of black and Creek dialect is indeed one of his greatest achievements.[5]

Posey's short stories "Uncle Dick's Sow," and "Mose and Richard" reveal how effectively Posey renders black dialect. In these trickster-like stories, the deep structure of the narrative subverts and radically interrogates the rules and structures of the dominant culture. Furthermore, given that Posey's stories are situated within the historical context of Indian Territory, it does not seem unusual that the central characters in both "Uncle Dick's Sow" and "Mose and Richard" are black men. In "Uncle Dick's Sow," Uncle Dick possesses a pig with a rebellious nature, and in the latter story Uncle Dick sends his two boys to school. Posey's use of black characters reflects the racial composition of his own Creek heritage and the dramatic population transfiguration of Indian Territory just prior to Oklahoma's statehood.

Posey's discourse with his black characters Uncle Dick, Uncle Will, Mose, Richard, and Aunt Cook represents Native people's fears, whether real or exaggerated, about the shrinkage of tribal lands and the loss of political power. The Native people's attempt to hold on to their position and, at the same time, not be the "other" reflects the complicated struggle with conflicting ideologies and the Native American's desire to maintain some degree of power.

Native people were afraid of losing their "place," which at best was precarious because of Euroamerican expansion into their lands. They were "allowed" to stay in the territories (where they had already experienced a diminishment in their position) by the sufferance of Euroamericans. Native peoples must have felt that the influx of "outside" blacks threatened even further what limited "place" they had. It is therefore little wonder that Native peoples were anxious and eager to displace their anxieties onto blacks, who up to this point had been "other" to Natives. Native people were threatened, they believed, by being doubly displaced from land and power. Posey senses these paradoxes and creates a means for his Native American audience to react to their own fears by displacing Native people's phobias, fears, and desires onto blacks.

Posey's strategy relies on the conventions of the Creek world. He wears the mask of the trickster, Chinnubbie Harjo, and lures the reader into accepting his paradoxical world, where trickster-like characters fool and warn their readers. Like Rabbit, who reveals a vast range of actions and emotions, Posey demonstrates in his stories the range of possibilities for Native Americans. At some points, he shows his people behaving like Euroamericans, at other times being aligned with blacks, and at times despising them. His position fluctuates and reflects the complicated nature of the changing world of Indian Territory. Posey's amusing, "simple" stories appear on the surface to render merely the flavor of his rural locale, but in fact they reveal a complex Creek culture that few people even today seem aware of. He speaks about his people as oppressors, as people who had their own prejudices about blacks and freedmen.

"Uncle Dick's Sow" deals with an uppity pig that belongs to Uncle Dick, who desperately tries to control her. His pig, though, breaks out of her pen and wanders off, eating the potatoes of Uncle Dick's friend, Uncle Will. Aggravated with this unruly pig, Uncle Will has his dog, "majah," chase the pig until she is captured. When Uncle Dick gets wind of what has happened to his prize pig, he seizes Uncle Will's musket, which is hanging over the door, and fires it over his friend's head. The story ends with Uncle Dick and Uncle Will's reconciliation, and the pig restored to her pen. The narrator sums up the pig's life:

> The sow's career thereafter was smooth and uneventful. Realizing that she was leading a bad life and being a wise sow, she resolved to cut loose from her wickedness, and she did. She became a devoted mother and replenished Uncle Dick's larder with numerous fat shoats—some of them weighing not less than fifty pounds. (33)

If we look closely at the pig's actions, we see that the pig plays out the contradictions as "other." The narrator alludes to the pig's exceptional characteristics, suggesting that she is radical, by equating her with a contemporary revolutionary figure, Emilio Aguinaldo, a Filipino freedom-fighter who was active during the Spanish-American War. The pig demonstrates her tendency to be transgressive, since she "wernt bo'n in no pen, kaze she lub liberty better'n de white folks" (32). Furthermore, like trickster, the pig reveals that she also has her own bag of tricks. The narrator continues, "Cunnie? She's cunnin's cousin Dick hiself an' dat's sho gibin' huh lots o' cunnin'!" (32).

It is significant that Posey identifies the pig with a non-Euroamerican hero, for the pig comes to represent Native people in the story. The narrator points to the rascally nature of Uncle Dick's pig and notes the difficulties of keeping this kind of "cunnin'" pig confined. Posey transforms the pig to signify the actions of Native people by further identifying the pig's actions and behaviors with her owner, Uncle Dick; she possesses a discriminatory palate, preferring such foods as yams and "roast'n' ears." In other words, the pig desires the food of blacks. Yet Posey reveals the transitory position of Native people when he also says that his pig "was no common sow. She had tastes approaching refinement" (32). Just as the pig is identified with blacks, she also desires to displace them.

The pig identifies with the manners and the practices of the dominant group, the Euroamericans, including their attitudes and beliefs about the "other." Uncle Dick's pig reveals her dislike for blacks as she announces her abhorrence of "sofkies." In order to understand Posey's encoded message that exposes his own people's fears about blacks, it is important to clarify how the word *sofky* is used in the context of this story. *Sofky*, a Creek word, denotes a traditional dish of hominy corn that Creeks are fond of eating. Posey relished this dish, but here it symbolizes much more than a Native delicacy, at least in Posey's mind: sofky becomes synonymous with Creek identity. He makes an interesting notation in his journal when his wife, Lowena, a non-Native American, learns how to make sofky:

> I must compliment my wife on the sofky she made today—this being her first effort. She, by some hook or crook, contrived to give it just the proper flavor. No one but an Indian can make sofky; Lowena can make sofky; therefore Lowena is an Indian! (Dale, 409)

Posey states that this word, *sofky,* became dramatically transposed: "sofky is a Creek word . . . but it has been corrupted by the white man and is made to denote a contemptible dog. Therefore, the sofkies . . . are pupy [*sic*], whelp and hound and curs of low degree" ("Uncle Dick's Sow," 33).

Even though the pig likes the foods of blacks, nonetheless she speaks derogatorily about them, aligning herself with Euroamericans as she calls blacks "sofkies." The narrator says that the pig's "attitude toward 'sofkies' in general was not calculated to breed familiarity. She despised them individually, collectively and as a race" (32). The pig thus does not identify with the commoners; she thinks of herself as being above the common "cur." In other words, the pig thinks of herself as above blacks. The pig, furthermore, shows aggressive behavior toward blacks. The narrator continues, "Nothing gave her [the pig] greater pleasure than to make a vain young cur run over himself" (32).

In effect, Native Americans' fears and anxieties are displaced onto blacks, even though Euroamericans were displacing Indian populations at a greater rate than were blacks. It is the Indians' perception of blacks moving into their position that Posey acts out in his story. Whether their misgivings were real or exaggerated, Indians in some way were threatened by blacks, perhaps fearing that they would become the "other" with blacks or perhaps become even *lower* than blacks. The narrator adds that the pig's obsession with such foods (black foods) inevitably leads to her downfall. For the narrator tells us "her fondness for these things (yams and roast'n' ears) brought about her undoing" (32). The narrator also warns his audience about transgressive behavior by alluding to what happens when Native people try to erase their "otherness" by desiring the "tastes" of blacks. The pig likes the foods of blacks, even as she allies herself with Euroamericans. Now, the narrator suggests, the pig devours blacks by ingesting their foods, and this leads to her "capture." Perhaps Posey is suggesting that if the pig (Native American) allies herself with Euroamericans, she too is in danger of being devoured. Posey uses this rebellious pig to skirt prescribed racial boundaries, signifying to Native people their own precarious position.

However, "Uncle Dick's Sow" concludes with Uncle Dick and Uncle Will corralling the pig back to her "place." The pig, in desiring forbidden food and putting down "curs," is punished for her unconventional behavior. Because the pig "lub liberty" and refused to sleep in her pen, or metaphorically overstepped preexisting racial lines, she "gave her neighbors something to talk about" (32). Uncle Will's dog, "majah," chases her until she is captured (but she doesn't avoid a violent confrontation with Uncle Will). With a bloody nose, the pig "grunting and in deep dejection, struck a bee line for home" (32).

Posey (re)produces a means for his predominantly Native American audience to react to their own fears and anxieties about their position as "other." He aligns the pig with a Filipino freedom-fighter, with blacks, and with Euroamericans. In the first instance Posey shows Native Americans breaking out of their position as "other." They must do so by devouring blacks. But Posey's ending suggests that this is not the action to take, for Uncle Will punishes the pig for her actions. Posey also shows the pig closely identifying with the actions and behaviors of blacks. Yet this position suggests that Native Americans will become more "invisible" if they are not distinct from blacks. Finally, Posey places his pig with Euroamericans, including their attitudes and beliefs about blacks. This position, of course, reveals dangerous assumptions about Native Americans' fears and desires concerning blacks. Posey, in "Uncle Dick's Sow," makes tracks across convoluted and ambiguous racial boundaries. Though he seems to vacillate, he persists in interrogating and critiquing existing racial stereotypes, reflecting the conflicting and paradoxical nature of Indian Territory.

Posey continues his trickster-like tactic of exposing people's fears of the "other" in the short story "Mose and Richard," which further interrogates the notion of hegemonic power. "Mose and Richard," although a comic story about two boys' mischievous escapades, reaffirms Native Americans' desires and fears about blacks and reveals how certain Native Americans felt about educating blacks. Many Native Americans greatly valued education, and writers such as Posey recognized the importance of establishing a literary space where Native American voices could be heard. This was Ora Eddleman Reed's desire as she published and brought to the foreground lesser-known Native American writers and poets in her magazine, *Twin Territories*. But Native American attitudes about educating blacks and former slaves varied. "Mose and Richard" deals with the controversy surrounding blacks and education as Posey unmasks his people's beliefs and anxieties about blacks.

In the story, Uncle Dick tells his two sons, Mose and Richard, that they must go to school, because as a former slave, he never had the opportunity to do so. On the first day of class, Uncle Dick takes Mose and Richard aside and tells them:

> I want you to learn somet'ing, kaze de time done git heah w'en if you grows up ignunt, de white man' an' Mistah Injin gwine to git de best ob you; an dey may git de best ob you anyhow, but hit aint gwine hu't you to go to school. (226)

Here, Uncle Dick exposes his position as being doubly oppressed by "de white man" and "Mistah Injin." But his words indicate that he is skeptical about getting out from under oppression; he does know, though, that education is a weapon that can perhaps change his boys' position.

Mose and Richard listen to their father's speech, but like most boys, they cannot stay out of trouble. Richard, the more mischievous of the two, comes home with a swollen lip and his shirt-sleeve ripped off. He barely survives the close scrutiny of Aunt Cook, who tells him, "yuse awful onminful," as he concocts a woeful tale of "de bresh whut try to hol' me we'n de ho'nets been git at me" (226) to conceal the fact that he had been fighting with his classmates. Richard continues to tell Aunt Cook tall tales about what transpired at school.

But the boys are more worried about what their father will say if he finds out about their transgressive behaviors at school. In order to placate Uncle Dick, Mose and Richard contrive stories about their school work. Before church every Sunday, Uncle Dick asks his boys to recite what they have learned at school:

> Richard opened his blue-back speller, wound one leg around the other and made out to spell "g-o go" and "h-o-g hog," allowing each letter plenty of territory. Mose, likewise, spelled "c-l-i-n-g cling."
> "Boys, dat's sho good," said Uncle Dick greatly pleased. (227)

At first impressed with his boys' learning, Uncle Dick soon realizes that they are playing tricks on him. On the third Sunday when he again asks Mose and Richard to recite to him their school learning, he knows that they have duped him. He asks Mose what he has learned and Mose replies: "'Doan know nut'n,' replied Mose, 'cep dat word c-l-i'" (228). When Uncle Dick finds out that instead of learning, his boys had been day-dreaming and fighting with their classmates, he sends both to work in the cotton fields. Uncle Dick is, of course, aggravated with their lack of academic progress; the story ends with his humorous but deadly harangue about their incompetency:

> "Mose!" interrupted Uncle Dick, "I has er notion to break yo' head an' be done wid you. . . . I talk to you an' talk to you . . . but hit ain't do no good. . . . I wants yo to take dem books to de teachah . . . an' cling to er plow Monday mawnin'. . . . er I'll cling to yo' back wid er stick!" (228)

In this story, Richard, in what Uncle Dick refers to as "tricks and debilment," shows one-upmanship in his ability, like trickster, to deceive Aunt Cook and Uncle Dick. Like trickster, who spends his time duping others and being duped himself, Richard and Mose are also being "duped" by mainstream society. They are being tricked out of a formal education; both boys, like their father, Uncle Dick, are the products of double colonization; that is, they are downtrodden both by the "white man" and "Mastah Injin."

Perhaps even more revealing is the implication that Native people assert political authority over blacks, since Uncle Dick refers to the Indian as "Mistah Injin" (Littlefield and Parins, "Short Fiction," 29). Uncle Dick tells his boys: "De fus t'ing you gwine know you grow up, an' if you caint hol' up yo' end wid de white man an' Mistah Injin, hit gwine be yo' own fault, kaze I sen' bof you to school an' gin you good advice" ("Mose and Richard," 226). Posey thus reaffirms blacks' position within the racial hierarchy as lower and undeserving. The boys have an opportunity for education and do not avail themselves of it. Posey may be attempting to put the blame for blacks' lack of education on themselves, not on the whites or Indians.

Posey's short story exposes the paradox of blacks as they vie for an equal position within the rapidly changing territory, but he also replicates some Native American readers' desires to keep blacks in their place. For Posey writes at a time when interracial tension had greatly accelerated, ending in what the local newspapers called a "race war" (Grinde and Taylor, 220). In "Mose and Richard," Posey, whether inadvertently or intentionally, places blacks into what many Native people viewed as their rightful position, as slaves, working the cotton fields. Furthermore, he shows his black characters, Mose and Richard, as unworthy of a proper education. Richard, like trickster, is too preoccupied with getting into trouble, and Mose is "lazy" and "easy-going." Posey, through his own trickster mask, reinforces many Native people's desires to separate themselves from blacks.

In both stories, we see that blacks definitely hold the position as the "other"—lower than Native Americans and perhaps even despised by them. In "Uncle Dick's Sow," through trickster-like strategies, Posey shows Native Americans trying to take on the actions and the behaviors of Euroamericans as they attempt to distance themselves from blacks and freedmen. In "Mose and Richard," Posey further exposes his own aversion, whether conscious or not, to empowering blacks through education and suggests that if blacks are educated they may pose a threat to Native people. Here, Posey seems to say that blacks, like his fictitious characters Mose and Richard, are not worthy of such endeavors. But in doing so, he exposes some negative and uncomplimentary beliefs about blacks and perhaps about his own people.

Posey's short stories reveal that he has undertaken a very "tricky discourse," a strategy that attempts to make his people visible and distinct, as he tries to confront and to arrest the negative imagery of Native peoples at the expense of his black brethren. It is a discourse that relies on trickster strategies and shows contradictions and vacillations in his own thinking. Posey, through trickster narratives, re-creates the reality of the Creek world—where black men and Creek pigs trick and warn and discard the conventions of society, with ambiguous results.

5

SPITTING OUT THE STORIES
Retelling Creek Verbal Traditions

Blackberry Bird told me . . .
speak the mystery words from
great conch shell—sing the songs
of the wind, the Turtle and the Gar
that never die.

—*Creek poet Louis Littlecoon Oliver*[1]

Posey enjoyed listening to Creek stories such as "The Man Who became a Snake," "Rabbit Steals Fire,"[2] and others that circulated among Creek communities. He recognized that stories about Rabbit and Wolf, or deceitful Opossum, were a means to understand how Creeks viewed their world. Not only did he hear many stories, but he also felt compelled to publish various tales such as "Fable of the Foolish Young Bear" or "A Creek Fable" in *Twin Territories* or the *Indian Journal*.[3] Just prior to his death in 1908, Posey discussed the possibility of assembling a collection of Creek folktales, commenting that he had "enough material for a thousand pages" (Littlefield, *Posey*, 257).

Posey's interest in Creek stories in some ways parallels the performance-centered approach to verbal traditions, which focuses on specific communicative events rather than investigating specific texts or scripts (Finnegan, 43). Posey was not merely interested in "rewriting" verbal traditions and thereby capturing the interdependence between stories and Creek social life; he wanted to get at the heart of Creek culture through storytelling. Like the current scholars who perceive "performance as a mode of communication," a way of sending and receiving messages, Posey felt a powerful connection to Creek stories—he felt their importance was so integral to his culture that he sought to record them, to make them accessible to a larger audience. It is particularly interesting that Posey's rendering of such stories reflects his sensitivity to the verbal artistry employed in storytelling events and to the interrelationship between the storyteller and his or her audience. Posey captures, especially in his story "Chinnubbie and the Owl," the dynamic aspects of verbal performance— the multiple "voices" embedded in a story, including the teller's voice and his or her commentary and evaluative remarks, the various characters' voices, and the audience's anticipated reaction to the story.

In order to examine the influence of Creek verbal traditions on Posey's writings, it is first important to situate the Creek storytelling tradition, exploring how such stories reflect Indian world-views. Creek beliefs and attitudes about their universe, for example, where people and animals came from, how various deities interact and treat people, or how humans are connected to their physical universe, are embodied in stories that are transmitted from one generation to another. These stories, as Joel Martin points out in *Sacred Revolt,* taught Creeks to "perceive the extraordinary in the ordinary, to spot the uncanny in the routine" (22). There are stories that tell about the creation of the world and the origin of corn and tobacco, about infamous warriors and prophets, and about various animals.

According to Louis Littlecoon Oliver, a Creek storyteller and author of *Chasers of the Sun: Creek Indian Thoughts,* a "psychic" distance separates Creeks from Euroamericans, for he believes that Indians are more "susceptible and sensitive to non-physical force" (25). Oliver illustrates his belief by relating a story his grandmother told him about an event that occurred during the Creeks' forced migration from their homeland. During the journey, his grandmother's clan, led by their medicine man, approached the rim of a steep and rocky canyon. Everything looked perilous for the Creeks, who had traveled for three of four days without food or other provisions, since their supplies had been confiscated by a group of white men disguised as United States cavalrymen. The medicine man gathered his people around a small fire and told them, "We cannot afford to go to the head of the canyon, but in order to escape the marauders, we must cross here" (26). Oliver concludes his story with his grandmother's remark: "it seemed that the canyon banks came together and they crossed over safely" (26). This comment appropriately acknowledges that the story lacks a satisfactory explanation for a large majority of Euroamericans: the account is unverifiable and therefore outside the realm of Euroamerican belief system—unless, of course, it can be equated to similar incidents recorded in the Koran or the Bible, for the merging of the canyon walls to let the Creeks pass across resembles Moses' parting of the Red Sea to lead his people from Egypt.

Like the Bible, which delineates the Western view of creation and other stories that govern Christian practices and beliefs, the telling of specific Creek stories recounts a similar religious system. Oliver's retelling of the inception of the world and the Great Spirit's purposes and sanctions is a detailed recounting of the time period before human creation.[4] It is apparent from Oliver's story that he perceives that everything in the world emanates from a supernatural power. Thus, objects such as rocks or plants or stones, which Western culture views as strictly nonsentient things, are considered conscious entities. John R. Swanton, an early ethnographer, notes this distinction between how Euroamericans view natural objects and how his informants ascribe characteristics to these things. Swanton states that entities received their living force back in time, somewhere near the beginning of creation (Swanton, *Religious Beliefs,* 489).

Another ethnographer of Southeast tribal peoples, James Mooney, focused on Cherokee myths and folktales, which resemble Creek oral tradition.[5] He records that Native peoples believe that animals at the time of creation were thought to be larger and a more "perfect type" than contemporary animals. Furthermore, Oliver says that this liminal period established the Creeks' spiritual connection to animals. According to Oliver, the Great Spirit instructed his people to allow the various animals that were seeking protection and food into their homes; the Indians welcomed the animals into their homes and thereby claimed a permanent relationship with them as a clan (Oliver, 5). At one time, Oliver states, there were a dozen or more clans, but only the Bear, Deer, Bird, Wind, Potato, Raccoon, and Panther (tiger) remain (5). Like the Creeks and their clans, mythical animals have chiefs, councils, and town houses, with each animal possessing a specific role within "animal society." For instance, Frog was the marshal and leader within the council, while Rabbit, the trickster, was the messenger and usually led the dances (Mooney, *Myths,* 231). It is not clear in what manner the animals came to be living on the earth, but it is believed they had come from the lower world, not migrating en masse, but each animal ascending in his own time (Oliver, 5; Mooney, *Myths,* 230).

In a world where animals in many ways mirror the actions and behaviors of humans, it does not seem unusual for animals to speak. Swanton records an incident where his informant, a prophet, overhears a conversation between an Owl and a Dog. According to the prophet, the Owl said:

"People must be afraid of me." The Dog answered his bird friend: "No, but if there is a big stick lying across the road they will be afraid of that." "Would they be afraid of a bush?" inquired the Owl. The Dog explains to the Owl: "They would not be afraid of that; they would go around it." Puzzled by his friend's remarks, the Owl persists in trying to understand "human logic." He asks the Dog: "But would they not be afraid if I should get up on top of the bush?" The Dog replies: "If you do it, they will kill you" (Swanton, *Religious Beliefs,* 489). The two "nonhuman" human observers continue their conversation for some time; finally, the owl perches himself on top of a bush in the middle of the road in an effort to try to scare any person who may pass along the road; his attempt, however, is not very fruitful (489).

This story, in some ways, is very puzzling. Owl, who is usually presented as the wise bird with all the answers, seems stupid in this context, since he cannot fathom why anyone would be startled by a stick. Dog, as man's companion, seems to understand the peculiar logic of humans, as he tries to explain to Owl that a human could mistake a stick for a snake. Dog continues to outline human logic as he carefully explains that a bush found in a person's path would give him no alarm—the person would simply go around it. Dog understands human logic, but Owl's confusion in trying to follow Dog's explanation reveals the stupid reasoning of humans. It makes no sense to Owl what humans fear.

Owl and Dog speak about human actions; Owl, in his own manner, attempts to bring humans down to earth as he tries to scare a human while he perches on top of a bush. Owl and Dog examine human actions and behaviors, giving us another perspective on our own humanness.

Talking owls occur frequently in the Creek verbal tradition. Oliver's poem "Hoot Owls Roast an Indian" focuses on the "talking Owls," who also comment on inane human behaviors. Oliver prefaces his poem, "I was camped on the Baron Fork crick when the following conversation of owls took place" (76). The speaker translates the owls' language, making it intelligible to his audience. In the first stanza, "Who who—whowho—ah!" becomes ("I've found an Indian in a whiteman's tent") (75; parentheses in original). The owls continue their conversation, "roasting" an Indian for his stupid actions as they mock, deride, and laugh at his attempt to catch a fish. Of course, the joke is that the owls discover that the man is not alone but in the company of a woman. One owl exclaims, "I'll bet a fat mouse he hasn't caught a fish, and don't expect to!!" Oliver's poem reveals the owls' playful, inquisitive nature as they attempt to discern what the human beings really are doing in the woods.

Another Creek story refers to the mythical time when human beings could communicate with animals. Here, though, the message is clearly that this is "dangerous" talk. In this story an old woman, frightened by the sight of a bellowing bull, tries to get out of his path. He, however, reassures her: "Don't be afraid of me. I am just enjoying my singing" (Swanton, *Myths*, 74). After he scares her, he adds that she must not tell anyone about what has just happened.

The woman goes about her usual business and, appreciative of her newly discovered talent, eavesdrops on her animal friends. She discovers that her chickens have contrived a plan to trick her out of more corn by scurrying over to her blind side and stealing the feed from her. The old woman is basically good-natured and simply finds their chicaneries to be amusing. She chuckles to herself about the mischief her chickens are creating. Meanwhile, her crotchety old man saunters into where she is feeding her chickens and thinks that she is giggling about another man. Of course, the old woman tries to explain to her husband her recent adventure with the bull and also tells him what her chickens have been saying. But before her words are even out of her mouth, she falls over dead (74). This story reveals an important transaction that should not be taken lightly: the old woman is giving messages away to her husband when she should not be. Even though it appears to be a harmless tale about an old woman and her clucking chickens, it clearly defines "speaking" as something that cannot transpire between animals and humans without sometimes causing fatal consequences.

Animals, however, can speak candidly about humans or can discuss almost anything among themselves. For example, Posey's story "The 'Possum and the Skunk" (or "How the 'Possum Lost the Hair Off His Tail") alludes to the time when animals were able to speak. The story begins, "When there were no monkeys with their tails stamped off calling themselves people, all the animals talked together." Opossum struts around boasting about his beautiful tail. He even loudly sings: "The 'possum has a bushy tail. The old skunk's tail is stick [*sic*] and pale."

However, Cricket, who crawls out from under a large black crevice, sees Skunk slinking around with downcast eyes, dejected and unable to bear Opossum's taunting. Cricket asks Skunk, "Why are all these tears?" Cricket then tells him: "Cheer up. I will put the fixings on the 'possum."

Cricket devises a plan whereby he later chews off Opossum's big bushy tail. The next day when Opossum goes about his usual ritual of displaying his gorgeous tail, he discovers it is missing, with "only the bare bone" remaining. Opossum faints, and Skunk carefully gathers up the fallen hair and takes it to Medicine Wolf, who fastens it onto the tail of Skunk. The story ends, "Ever since then the skunk has carried a busy tail and the 'possum has worn a habitual grin."

Posey's story is a familiar tale, one that circulates among Creek storytelling circles,[6] in which Opossum, Skunk, and Cricket play out a recurring social situation that mimics human behavior. Opossum tries to separate, and even elevate, himself from other animals; in other words, he attempts to assert his individualism as represented by his obsession with his "fine bushy tail." He brags incessantly about its outstanding qualities; his assertions intimidate and undermine Skunk, who feels inadequate because of his own puny tail.

In Creek culture, excessive individualism threatens collaboration, an ethic important to group cohesiveness. In this story, therefore, Opossum is punished for his anti-collective behavior. Moreover, his punishment is unanimously administered by the cooperative actions of Skunk, Medicine Wolf, and Cricket, who all bring about his downfall.

By listening to "animal talk," Creeks learn that the song and speech of Opossum are not acceptable nor socially sanctioned and even may bring about terrible consequences. Posey, like may of his fellow Creeks, enjoyed the overturning of Opossum. On the surface, stories such as this seem innocent and purely entertaining, but they also illustrate Creek beliefs and attitudes. The structure of animal society, after all, parallels Creek society, with each animal having a designated role and place. For instance, Opossum's behavior demonstrates what happens if a person sings too loudly about his or her own qualities.

Some Native American cultures such as the Zuni have definite restrictions on storytelling. For example, the Telapnaawe, Zuni stories similar to Creek animal stories, can be told only from October to March, "lest the narrator be bitten by a snake, and only at night, lest the sun set early" (Tedlock, xvi). Some Creek stories also appear to have particular parameters that determine when they can be told. For example, Swanton's informant, Sam Watt, asserts that particular stories, including tales about cannibals and the tie-snake, could only be told during cold weather, or "otherwise bad luck would follow" (Swanton, *Myths*, 20). In contrast,

Cherokee stories can be told day or night and during any season (Mooney, *Myths,* 232). Whereas each culture has its particular time when stories can or cannot be told, most cultures have conventional formulas that trigger the coming of a story. Euroamericans sense the advent of a story when they hear "Once upon a time"; similarly, Creek or Cherokee storytellers begin with the words "This is what the old men told me when I was a boy" (232).

"Chinnubbie and the Owl," another story written by Posey, reproduces the social context of Creek storytelling, where the narrator focuses on describing the event. After introducing Chinnubbie as an "extraordinary" storyteller, the narrator goes on to say, "It was in the twilight of a lovely summer day, while the chiefs, medicine men, and warriors were grouped in a circle around the blazing campfire, discussing the success of a recent chase, parleying over various topics, and relating numerous anecdotes, that the prophet arose and offered a costly bow and twelve arrows to the one who could relate the best story of his experience, or the best he could make on the spur of the moment." The narrator captures the moment when storytelling occurs. He situates his storytelling in the evening, when stories were frequently told. According to Cherokee storyteller John Axe, storytellers and priests gathered in the "asi," a low, log sleeping house. Here, in the comfort of a blazing fire, the men would gather in a circle "to recite the traditions and discuss their secret knowledge" (230). Sometimes a young boy was asked to tend the fire, and he was then able to listen to the stories and learn something of the sacred rites performed by the men. This is how Axe learned to be an adept storyteller. Customarily, the boy placed several pine knots upon the coals, and here he would sit listening to the men tell numerous stories (230).

The situation in "Chinnubbie and the Owl" resembles John Axe's storytelling experience; in this story, the warriors, chiefs, and medicine men congregate around a fire, with each man waiting his turn to tell his favorite story. The art of storytelling is a theme that weaves it way into "Chinnubbie and the Owl," for the narrator also stresses the performative aspect of storytelling, since the prophet offers a bow and twelve arrows to the person who performs the best story. "Chinnubbie and the Owl" reveals, at least in Posey's terms, what exactly constitutes a "good" story. The narrator brings to the foreground the spontaneity of storytelling, in this case Chinnubbie's ability to concoct a wonderful tale. The narrator thus notes the performative element of storytelling, stressing the oral nature of a "talking" story.

Chinnubbie is a teller of "extraordinary merit." When he spoke, "his hearers gave strict attention for there was a charm in his speech that was truly admirable, and something in his eloquent wit that captivated the gravest of his audience." Ever ready to spin an exciting tale, Chinnubbie could not resist the challenge of a contest. As he jumps up from his "grassy lounge," he utters his favorite phrase, "By the bears, I wish a part in this myself."

The storytelling contest that frames the narrative of "Chinnubbie and the Owl" enables Chinnubbie to tell his story and also mirrors Creek verbal tradition. A teller gains the attention of his audience and thus proceeds to recount his story. According to Swanton, the Creeks perceive a story as something that is literally "spit out" from the storyteller's mouth. Swanton explains that "when a storyteller finished his narrative he would spit, and then another would have to contribute a story in return, and in this way the cue was taken up by one after another until the 'children went to bed'" (Swanton, *Religious Beliefs,* 521).

Along with the idea of Chinnubbie poised, ready to "spit out" his story to his audience, the narrator notes that the storytellers had "plucked a gem from memory's treasury of old traditions to veneer the imperfect portions of their unpremeditated story." In other words, the stories that were told were familiar to the audience, derived from Creek verbal tradition, but each teller simply had "reinvented" or "refashioned" a story, making it his own. Thus the stories that Chinnubbie and the other storytellers relate connect them to their oral tradition, to their people.

Unlike literate-oriented cultures that regard authors as owners or creators of their own fictions, Creeks and other oral cultures consider stories communal property. Stories are handed down from one generation to another and transmitted orally—no one "owns" these stories. Siquanid, a Cherokee storyteller, speaks about the importance of storytelling in his own community: "The things they told long ago are very interesting to hear. It is almost impossible to remember it [what was told] all. It seems that one can remember only a small amount of it. When people can remember all of it, they can tell very interesting things" (Kilpatrick, 4). Siquanid suggests that most Cherokees are familiar with the their own verbal tradition, yet he does emphasize that not everyone is a "natural" storyteller. Siquanid continues: "Many people do not tell the stories right: they get them all mixed up. That is the reason why these stories sometimes vary. Some people know more of the stories, some less" (5). Similarly, Mooney notes that most of the animal stories are familiar to nearly everyone and are found in almost identical versions among the Creek as well as the Cherokee and other southern tribes (*Myths*, 231). Stories thus circulate freely and are widely dispersed, crossing over traditional tribal boundaries.

Posey also alludes to the repertoire of Creek stories that his people know as he constructs a narrative frame that places Chinnubbie about to embark upon his story that wins the storytelling contest and the admiration of his listeners. The narrator indicates that Chinnubbie's story relies on oral tradition when he states that the more a story is told the "more attractive it becomes." Chinnubbie says that he is about to tell a "true" experience. Moreover, he signifies to his listeners that what he really will impart is something familiar to them. He suggests that the older a story is, the "more attractive" it becomes, because it is more established in tradition. He also points out that stories are only preserved if they are told frequently, making them firmly secure in tradition. In a clear and articulate manner, then, the narrator imparts his beliefs about the oral transmission of stories.

But as many Indian writers point out, a story becomes new each time it is told, bringing fresh meaning to the teller and audience. Chinnubbie begins his story: "It has been quite awhile since this incident, which I am about to relate to you, was experienced. But warriors, a good story, however ancient, is always new, and the more frequently told, it is destined to never be obliterated from the memory in which it lives." He further mentions the important role that stories play: they bring comfort to their listeners, and "the mind is released from the bonds of its cares and solitudes." Attempting to entice us into his story, he says that it is as "an evergreen in my recollections." Chinnubbie also believes that his story is unique and will have a lasting influence on his audience.

Chinnubbie alludes to the necessity of keeping the stories alive because people derive meaning from retelling stories. Leslie Marmon Silko also speaks about the importance of stories to her own Puebloan people. She says that "the stories are always bringing us together, keeping this whole together, keeping the family together, keeping the clan together" (59). She goes on to say that a person does not get well alone, "but it is together, in our stories and storytelling, that we look after each other and take care of each other." Her words are applicable to all Native American cultures, including the Creeks. Like Silko, Posey realizes the important role stories play in his own Creek culture.

Yet whereas Silko stresses the healing aspect of storytelling, Chinnubbie explains to his listeners that he tells his story only to his most intimate friends, cautioning them not to repeat it, "as it would doubtless excite the jealousy of the prophets," who, he feels, are his "superiors in the creation of such narratives." In his boastful way, Chinnubbie focuses on the powerful effect that storytelling can incite in its listeners. He entices his audience by suggesting that he has a new story to relate, a special story containing transformational powers. Next, he compares its power to the "conjuring" power that prophets can evoke, suggesting that stories reside in the realm of the supernatural. But, Chinnubbie continues, he is not certain whether his listeners will enjoy his story; nevertheless he chooses to "spit [it] out."

Chinnubbie tells about his experience in a foreign land, where he became lost and wandered into a hideous place teeming with "ferocious beasts and reptiles." Even in the noonday "its vast interior seemed dark and dusky with only a sunbeam here and there to illuminate its gloom." Chinnubbie ambles around without rest or food, until he encounters a peculiar owl; he stares at its countenance and thinks about the many eerie childhood stories that he has heard about such owls while he stands "bewitched and motionless in a trance of awe and silence." The owl grows to an enormous size.

When Chinnubbie later regains his senses, he interrogates the owl, demanding that he identify himself. The owl, however, merely mimics Chinnubbie's actions. Undaunted by the owl's enigmatic reply, Chinnubbie asks again: "Answer, by the bears and all beside, who are you?"

Finally, it becomes apparent to Chinnubbie that he is not making headway with this bothersome owl; he thus devises a plan to trick this strange bird. Slowly Chinnubbie begins circling the owl, who still persists in mimicking his actions by turning his head, without moving his body. By continually circling the owl, Chinnubbie manages to make it twist its head off, where it falls on the ground, telling him, "Take my head and place it in your belt, it will guide you to your home in safety!"

Chinnubbie obeys the owl's command and, fastening the head to his belt, arrives home without any further complications. At the conclusion of the story, Chinnubbie is met with hearty applause from his audience, and the prophet presents him with the bow and twelve arrows. However, Chinnubbie, being a great storyteller, has fabricated an "elaborate lie," making his audience believe that his story was based on personal experience.

Instead, he spins a story on the spur of the moment that captivates the attention of his audience. After the feast and other celebratory activities, Chinnubbie departs from his comrades, intent on another journey to "he knew not where, but leaving the impression that this object was to search the worlds in quest of spoils." Many years later Chinnubbie once again returns to his country. He is warmly greeted, and his people prepare a feast and other activities to celebrate his homecoming.

"Chinnubbie and the Owl" is a story embedded with other stories. Not only does the narrator tell a story about "storytelling" as a story within a story, but he also informs his audience about the mysterious owl, signifying on other Creek stories. The narrator leads his audience into the world of storytelling where one story conjures up the stories of another story. The process is never-ending: Chinnubbie ventures out into foreign lands, returning with yet another "story."

Thus storytelling presents infinite possibilities, numerous combinations of other story references that become enmeshed into a new story frame. The narrator tries to close his story, but it seems almost impossible to do so. The story ends with Chinnubbie's words not quite "spit out." The narrator mentions Chinnubbie's return and the fabulous feasting that occurs; he also alludes to Chinnubbie's oratory skills in "some blood-stirring philosophies." But the narrator cannot find the words to finish his story. He laments Chinnubbie's new stories: "but tradition has unfortunately failed to embalm them in its unwritten volumes." He suggests that Chinnubbie's stories resist the written word, leaving his intent "out there," unformulated. Indirectly, then, he alludes to the continuous process of storytelling, where words cannot be bound into volumes.

In an effort to get the story going, "Chinnubbie and the Owl" sidetracks into the folds of another story; in another instance, the stories seem to pile up on one another, as when Chinnubbie refers to his childhood stories about owls that have mystical functions. When Posey evokes the image of an enormous owl, he calls forth other "owl stories" circulating among Creek communities. The story structure of "Chinnubbie and the Owl" replicates what Silko refers to when she says that "often the speakers or tellers go into stories of the words they are using to tell one story so that you get stories within stories" (36).

Asudi, a ninety-two-year-old Cherokee storyteller, aptly demonstrates the embedded nature of storytelling as he recalls the old storytellers he remembers:

There are some things I do remember of the events of long
ago that they told about, these events that they passed down.
"Everything is just as God planned. He made everything the way
it is, and He planned the way all things should live"—that's what
they talked about. And they also included comical things in their
talks. In their conversations they would come to these jokes and
then go back to more serious things. They would continue and
say, "This is what he did; this is what he'll do; this is what he did;
this what he'll do; this is what he did." They would ask, "Who
started that?" There was always someone who knew, and he
would answer instantly. That's the way you heard things, and if
you didn't pay any attention, you wouldn't know anything. If
you had paid attention, you would know. (Kilpatrick, 5)

Asudi speaks about the nature of storytelling and how stories are woven
into the fabric of other stories. Thus stories give structure to the world and
enable people to have some sort of internal reference to sort out their per-
sonal experiences, for some story always touches upon something that
sounds familiar or reminds us of something that happened to someone we
know. As Asudi notes, stories include a wide range of telling activities, such
as myths that tell the way the world was created, or comical events like the
numerous tales of Opossum and Skunk, or what Silko refers to as "family
stories"—stories we tell others about our relatives or our ancestors. All of
these different kinds of narratives bind people together.

Stories, then, are often the cohesive "glue" that gives people important
references for how to act or to behave. Silko uses the example of when
someone's old uncle does something irreverent to demonstrate the use-
fulness of keeping a story "going." "In other words," Silko explains, "this
process of keeping track, of telling, is an all-inclusive process which begins
to create a total picture" (58). It is crucial to know all of the stories in order
to protect a person from someone who is an enemy of the family. A person
may hear a "version" of his uncle's unacceptable behavior that, for instance,
does not sound plausible, perhaps a story that does not even show his
uncle in a favorable light. Then this "telling" would reveal an enemy.

Silko believes that if a person keeps very close watch, "listening con-
stantly to learn the stories about other families, one is in a sense able to deal
with terrible sorts of things that might happen within one's own family"
(58–59). There is never simply "one story," but numerous variants of that

story, told by different families of storytellers; in other words, no person or family "holds" all the stories, nor is anyone alone in his or her stories. It is only in the unraveling of each story that we obtain a more enlightened view of the total collage of stories.

Stories help us understand our life experiences and, as Silko notes, guide us through horrendous situations. There is always someone else's family with an uncle or brother who did something even more horrid than one's own uncle did. Or there is someone like Chinnubbie who tells an "unexcusable falsehood." Posey's story "Chinnubbie and the Owl" invites other possibilities of combining traditional stories into new narratives, suggesting the never-ending process of storytelling. He leaves his listeners thinking that around the next corner is another "good" story.

Posey's "rewriting" of traditional Creek stories such as "The 'Possum and the Skunk" or his "own" story, "Chinnubbie and the Owl," captures many different facets of storytelling. Posey was intrigued with the human-like qualities of Opossum and Skunk and all the other animals he knew from the Creek verbal tradition. It is evident that "Chinnubbie and the Owl" resembles in many ways folkloric animals and their actions.

Posey also tries to recreate how storytelling works within Creek culture—that a story may not have meaning until it is told and played out in another context. He aptly shows that meaning and reality are constantly in flux, continuously being reevaluated and incorporated into another story. This is a central theme that is derived from Native Americans' sense of orality: a person always searches for new meaning in a story; as a story is retold, it gathers a different significance.

Like Posey, Silko explains the importance of storytelling in Puebloan culture: "'Don't go away, don't isolate yourself, but come here, because we have all these kinds of experiences'—this is what the people are saying to you when they tell you these other stories" (59). Like the people from Silko's Laguna Pueblo, Chinnubbie cannot leave his people, or at least not for very long, because eventually he must return and spin another "good" story. Both Posey and Silko believe that stories bring people together, linking them to their traditions, to their families, to their selves. People find their way through stories that knot or relink them with a tribal identity, enabling them to reclaim their communal self.

6

THE BIRTH OF HOTGUN, TOOKPAFKA MICCO, AND OTHER NOTABLE CREEK CHARACTERS

> *Crow, in the new snow.*
> *You caw, caw*
> *like crazy.*
>
> *Laugh.*
> *Because you know I'm a fool*
> *Too, like you*
> *skimming over the thin ice*
> *to the war going on*
> *all over the world.*
> —*Creek poet Joy Harjo*[1]

"One of the best ways to understand a people is to know what makes them laugh," writes Vine Deloria (146). In a discussion of Indian humor, he writes that many non-Indians, especially so-called "professed" experts, skim the top of Native American cultures, not detecting and therefore not appreciating an essential component that glues Native cultures together. "I sometimes wonder how," Deloria continues, "anything is accomplished by Indians because of the apparent overemphasis on humor within the Indian world. Indians have found a humorous side of nearly every problem and the experiences of life have generally been so well-defined through jokes and stories that they have become a thing in themselves" (146–47).

Deloria's observations about Indians and humor parallel those of Louis Littlecoon Oliver, a Creek who grew up in Coweta, Oklahoma. Oliver comments that Creeks "cannot discuss any serious matters without allowing humor to intervene" (54). Furthermore, he states that the inclination to find a humorous side to any matter, even a situation that many people from other cultures would not think of as appropriate for joking, is a Creek tendency. "It is known that in the old days in Creek court sessions and trials," Oliver remarks, "the questioning by lawyers and interpretations by interpreters brought on much roaring laughter" (54). Humor is highly valued, and almost every person is "a clown unto himself verbally" (53). Oliver explains the role that humor plays in his own community:

> So where ever the Creeks meet, whether in twos, fours or a crowd, there will be chuckles, laughter, and at times roaring laughter. There may be an old stonefaced Creek leaning on his cane as people pass by. Be assured he is smiling inwardly of something funny that he saw. When he tells it to his friends, there will be, in unison, a thunderous roar of laughter. (54)

As noted in chapter 5, Creek stories, as well as Posey's rewriting of these stories, sometimes create funny incidents that point out human vulnerability as personified by Opossum, Skunk, and other animal characters. Opossum's bungling represents human beings' ability to wreak havoc on life. Thus humor seems close to the surface, ready to erupt, refashioning almost anything that Creeks have an occasion to tell. Counteracting bitter cultural memories wrought by colonization, humor binds people together; or as Kenneth Lincoln contends, it takes some of the "fatal sting out of history" (55). Whatever one believes, humor is integral to a Native American perspective.

Posey's Fus Fixico letters, published from October 1902 to May 1908—appearing sometimes regularly and at other times more sporadically in various territorial newspapers, including the *Indian Journal,* the *Fort Smith Times,* the *Muskogee Evening Times* (formerly the *Muskogee Morning Times*), and the *Muskogee Phoenix*[2]—portray a humorous side to Indian life and Indian-Euroamerican relations. "Fus Fixico," a name that some have translated as "heartless bird," "repeats" what he overhears discussed by several Creek full bloods, such as Hotgun, Tookpafka Micco, Wolf Warrior, and Kono Harjo.

The "talk" of Fus and his friends is modeled after conventional Creek speech patterns. They mull over the political happenings in Indian Territory, deciding what they can playfully deride within the parameters of socially accepted talk. Their speech literally treads the line between what is considered funny and that which is dangerous. First we will examine Posey's development of Fus, his own persona, along with several other characters whom he tests out in his letters, as he tries to create an amalgamation of narrative voices. Posey's literary success is partly achieved by establishing comic dialogue within a familiar cultural setting that we will examine in some detail. Within this traditional atmosphere, talk occurs—talk that mirrors and reinforces tribal solidarity. Lastly, in order to understand how Fus and his friends negotiate their liminal position, we will investigate their conversation, considering more closely the kinds of criticism and jokes that they make.

During the course of the letters, Fus's own voice fades into the margins, while Hotgun and Tookpafka Micco become animated, comic commentators, making observations about juicy tribal gossip. Sometimes their remarks target events outside their immediate domain, such as the controversy about statehood; Hotgun and Tookpafka are well-informed Indians, even voicing strong opinions about such faraway places as Japan and Russia.

Fus and his intimate circle of full-blooded Creek friends smoke, spit, and eat sofky and other Creek delicacies while chatting about local happenings. At times, Fus is so busy that he is barely able to report on the local gossip, as when he admits: "I didn't had no time to write. My cotton was bust open so much last two three weeks I was to pick it out like everything" (Littlefield and Hunter, *Fus*, 55); at other times Fus becomes preoccupied with his own affairs, rambling on about his recent harvest. Fus shows his own prejudice about blacks: "I was raise about two wagons plum full of sofky corn too, and lots of bushels of sweet potatoes, like what the white mans call 'nigger chokers'—they wont choke Injins though, 'cause Injins don't eat potatoes that was cooked dry like niggers" (56). Fus assumes that his joke is harmless, revealing his animosity toward blacks as he describes potatoes the choke "niggers" while "Injins" survive. One of the bitter ironies about Fus's joke, of course, is that black freedmen composed a large segment of the marginalized Creek population. But it is evident that Fus does not see blacks as "Injins."

Not only does Fus "overhear" and thus report gossip and his own prejudices, but along with other Creek characters he discusses and makes jokes about the graft and shady dealing of various politicians who vie for control over Indian allocations, cutting deals with their cronies, while Indian leaders such as Creek Indian chief Pleasant Porter wield their own power. All this is discussed and turned into playful, but frequently caustic, judgments. Posey's weapon is laughter as he tears at the heart of political happenings in Indian Territory. Fus is Posey's own invented "fearless bird," subverting and exposing the inner workings of the political and economical shifting occurring in Indian Territory.

Like oral stories that enable people to cope with disruptive and potentially dangerous events, Posey's creation, the collective of Fus and his Creek friends, enables Creeks and other Native peoples to make sense of their world. Leslie Silko, as well as other Native American writers, recognizes the transformational power of such stories. She says that there is a way to tell things "so people can kind of laugh or smile. I mean, I'm really aware of the ways of saying things so you don't offend somebody, so you keep their interest, so you can keep talking to them. Often times these things are told in a humorous way" (Coltelli, 147).

By choosing the appropriate voice for his Fus Fixico letters, Posey "reads" Indian Territory and tunes his readers into the contradictions and paradoxes of Indian life.[3] Fus becomes a detached persona, reporting on tribal happenings and other political affairs. But Fus is not Posey's most powerful voice. An effective literary character would be an important key to Posey's Fus Fixico letters, but it would take him some time to develop.

Based on a real person, a Creek medicine man and member of the House of Kings (the Creek upper legislative body), Choela is one of Posey's early characters. Fus says about Choela:

> Old Choela was sure good doctor. He was just take his grubbing hoe and go out into the woods and dig up lots of medicine anywhere. Then he was take his cane and blow in the medicine pot long time and sing little song with it too, like at busk ground. But he aint want no monkey business round there neither while he was fixing that medicine. If you aint dead yet before he was got through, he make you so well you just want lots of sofky. (Littlefield and Hunter, *Fus*, 53)

Perhaps Posey felt that Choela was too busy working his medicine to provide a strong voice for his Fus Fixico's letters. Maybe Choela, a traditional Creek steeped in the art of conjuring, did not see life as Posey wished to recreate it for Indian Territory. Posey, however, must have pondered for some time his move to eliminate his medicine man, since Choela becomes ill at least twice. Fus reports that "Choela was on sick list, but he get off pretty soon, I think. He was lay up and take his own medicine about three weeks maybe (E-mak-pof-ket)".[4] For whatever reason, Posey "kills" Choela in spring 1903. Fus, the harbinger of Creek gossip, tells his readers:

> Well, so I was tell you bad news about my old friend Choela. He was gone to be good Injin, like whiteman say when Injin die. It as

look like all old Injins die now and make good Injin that way.
Maybe so pretty soon Fus Fixico was make good Injin, too.
(Littlefield and Hunter, *Fus*, 76)

With the death of Choela, Fus listens to and relays more and more of Hotgun and Tookpafka Micco's conversations. Like Choela, Hotgun is created from a Creek full-blood, a follower of Chitto Harjo, whom Posey knew and interviewed (Littlefield, *Posey*, 167). Posey describes Hotgun as a Renaissance Indian, "an Indian tinkerer of great fame" who could do just about anything: "He was a philosopher, carpenter, blacksmith, fiddler, clockmaker, worker in metals and a maker of medicines" (167).

Hotgun has a flair for seeing and expressing the humorous side of life. Part of this comes from his ease with himself and his security with own his identity. Nothing is left unturned while he looks for playful moments—otherwise, he could not be the target of his own jokes. Hotgun jokes about the possibility of abandoning his own name—an act that most people, including Creeks, would not dare to joke about. On a particularly cold and bitter night Fus reports Hotgun's insights: "Hotgun he say it was get so cold last Sunday night he was had notion to change his name. I say him what he calls himself then and he say Blowgun was have more truth to it than Hotgun Sunday night when the wind was keep on blowing the rags out of the cracks in his cabin" (Littlefield and Hunter, *Fus*, 69). Hotgun enjoys his own pun and, more than anyone, seems pleased with his new name.

Hotgun, however, is not a stand-up comedian, rattling off jokes to a captive audience; his powerful voice merges with that of his cohort, Tookpafka Micco. Also based upon a real person, Tookpafka Micco puns along with Hotgun, adding further comic insights as both Indians reflect and comment on Creek life. Gerald Vizenor, known for his trickster novels, believes that the comic spirit is built around a collective model. He says: "You can't act in a comic way in isolation. You have to be included. There has to be a collective of some kind" (Bruchac, 295). Fus Fixico's letters become powerful as Creek voices commingle to bring humorous insights into some very tricky tribal and territorial happenings. Like Laurel and Hardy or Lucy and Ethel, Hotgun and Tookpafka Micco are a comic duo fueled by their unique relationship.

Hotgun and Tookpafka Micco anticipate one another's thoughts and thereby extend each other's puns; in almost every instance they are comically in sync. There is only one time where Tookpafka asks his partner to help him "read" a situation. Tookpafka says to Hotgun: "Well, so you was had to sight me" (Littlefield and Hunter, *Fus,* 140). But it only takes a moment for Tookpafka to determine the direction of Hotgun's thoughts; in his next reply, he has "sighted" the conversation, playing off Hotgun's comments. Hotgun and Tookpafka Micco's humor only succeeds when they are able to collaborate their ideas, mirroring each other's beliefs. This is what makes their words particularly amusing and demonstrates the importance of multiple voices that evolve from Creek verbal tradition.

Hotgun and Tookpafka's conversations with Wolf Warrior and Kono Harjo[5] are usually associated with food events, which inspire their thought-provoking talks. While Kono Harjo's wife or other Creek women pound sofky corn, a down-home powwow evolves. Most occasions center around Christmas or New Year's Day or simply evolve as spontaneous gatherings of the four friends. During these times, Hotgun or his sidekick Tookpafka Micco casually bring up the current gossip that surfaces around their homes, or perhaps their talk turns to a recent political maneuver of "Tams Big Pie" (Tams Bixby, chairman of the Dawes Commission) or "Secretary It's Cocked" (Ethan Allen Hitchcock, secretary of the interior), notorious politicians and favorite targets for ridicule. Fus describes a typical occasion:

> So it was Hotgun he had the women folks make some sour bread an' some blue dumpling an' some hick'ry nut sofky an' some good sak-ko-nip-kee[6] an' lots o' ol' time dishes like that for New Year. Then he invite his frien's to come an' feast with him. Tookpafka Micco he was there, an' Wolf Warrior he was there, an' Kono Harjo he was there. They was all come soon an' bring their folks an' dogs an' stayed till put near sun down. Hotgun he was had a little white jug sittin' back under the bed to' liven the conversation. (54)

Often times the four friends sit around someone's fireplace and light up their pipes. Sometimes, Hotgun "smoke slow an' look'way off in the Injin summer long time," or someone else spits in the ashes and says, "Well, so," signifying another talk. Usually the men's conversation meanders like a slow-moving creek, slipping through the valleys and nooks of Indian-Euroamerican politics.

During more affable weather, the four friends congregate outside, sometimes leaning their hickory chairs against a "catapa" tree as they conduct their powwow. Most times Wolf Warrior and Kono Harjo simply grunt, reaffirming anything and everything that their two friends, Hotgun or Tookpafka Micco, relate. Once in a while, Wolf Warrior asks a question or participates in the conversation, but usually both remain silent; this, however, does not mean their presence is not crucial. By "giving a big grunt" or spitting in the ashes of a fire or leaning forward in order to "pay close attention," they signify approval and affirmation.

Perhaps Wolf Warrior and Kono Harjo "pay attention" because Hotgun and Tookpafka Micco's dialogue treads a delicate line between overt criticism of Indian-Euroamerican politics and playful judgments. Their feigned "inability" to understand Euroamerican culture, like Tookpafka's anxiety about where he should spit his tobacco in a first-class train car, parodies the stereotypical "Injin" who cannot comprehend civilized behavior; of course, the "joke" is that Tookpafka Micco ridicules Euroamerican customs by disguising himself as a simple "Injin" who cannot read the dominant culture's behaviors. Hotgun and Tookpafka Micco tease their way into situations, framing their words into "harmless" observations about various political events occurring in Indian Territory.

Another reason perhaps that Wolf Warrior and Kono Harjo decide to "pay attention" to Hotgun and Tookpafka's talk is that they recognize this kind of playful judgment as something meaningful. Deloria states that teasing is a traditional Native American way of exacting social control and ensuring stability within a group. He says that "rather than embarrass members of the tribe publicly, people used to tease individuals they considered out of step with the consensus of tribal opinion" (147). James Welch also believes that teasing is an important element in Indian cultures; he states that it is "based on presenting people in such a way that you're not exactly making fun of them, but you're seeing them for what they are" (Coltelli, 192). Teasing is thus a tactful but playful way to reduce the other's game to what it really is.

Adept and crafty "tease meisters," Hotgun and Tookpafka Micco penetrate and expose Euroamerican games. They perform an artful juggling act that requires them to "sight" and play off each other's words, an act that also relies on their ability to stay within the parameters of comic playfulness. For however amusing Hotgun and Tookpafka Micco's comments may be, they are always at the expense of someone else. Keith Basso states, in his study of western Apache joking, that "there is always a possibility that persons who appear to be joking may not be joking at all" (69).

According to Basso, this is why Apaches often remark that joking can be "dangerous" (69). Thus Hotgun and Tookpafka Micco's jokes are always located elsewhere; the "danger" of their words lies underneath the surface as they deride and ridicule white politicians and their policies.

Freud also notes, in *Jokes and Their Relation to the Unconscious,* that jokes sometimes represent a "rebellion against authority, a liberation from its pressure" (105). In other words, jokes allow us to ridicule someone or something without calling attention to our motives, for jokes permit us to articulate seemingly inappropriate expressions. Freud states, "By making our enemy small, inferior, despicable, or comic, we achieve in a round-about way the enjoyment of overcoming him" (103). It thus becomes clearly evident that the line between overt derision and playful joking is very precarious.

Hotgun and Tookpafka Micco tread this line when Fus recounts how the "Big Man from Washington," Secretary It's Cocked, responds after he sees numerous "flimsy shacks" with side rooms erected by non-Indians, who rent land from the Creeks. Allotment leases required that the lessee improve the property, but at the expiration of the lease, the building structures became the property of the Indians. "Big Man" becomes so aggravated with what he sees that he snaps his cigar in two while he exclaims: "Well, so it's only a shack. I was druther had a dugout or maybe so a wagon sheet to live in" (Littlefield and Hunter, *Fus,* 96). He makes a mental note that he must make "some strong rules and regulations against that kind of thing on Injin land" (96).

Hotgun thinks for a moment. He says: "Maybe so Secretary It's Cocked was out of humor 'cause he didn't run onto some wigwams" (96). Taking his signal from Hotgun, Tookpafka Micco replies, "[It's Cocked] was thought all the time a box house with a side room to it was more respectable and civilized than log huts 'cause that's the only kind a house white people was stuck on" (96).

Hotgun and Tookpafka construct a scenario replete with culturally specific meanings. First, Hotgun draws attention to Secretary It's Cocked's humorless pose, which sets him apart from Indians, placing him in the position of other. From Hotgun and Tookpafka Micco's perspective, It's Cocked's behavior clearly is not appropriate. Furthermore, Hotgun also alludes to Indian stereotyping by bringing forth It's Cocked's belief that all Indians live in "wigwams." Hotgun rips apart a popular Euroamerican image, giving his partner room to expand on his comic perspective.

Tookpafka adds to Hotgun's comments by pointing his readers to the bitter irony of the situation; he interrogates the logic behind supposed Euroamerican superiority. Because government regulations require leasers to improve their leased land, "flimsy" shacks, which Secretary It's Cocked despises, have been built. As Tookpafka tells us, Indian housing structures, built from logs, are more sturdy and durable than the Euroamerican modeled shacks.

Hotgun and Tookpafka reveal several incongruities by bringing into focus, through playful joking, commonly held Euroamerican cultural codes, values, and norms. Wigwams, flimsy shacks, and log cabins collide with one another on the Indian landscape. Hotgun and Tookpafka Micco reveal the paradoxes of working out discursive practices in a space that contains/holds different cultural meanings. It is an intricate, complicated world where Hotgun and Tookpafka skate across cultural boundaries.

But both characters are not always intent on making sardonic comments about Indian-Euroamerican politics. Sometimes their chats simply are playful and full of hyperbole, like a trickster bragging about how many ducks he can eat. Both can deliver a story that thrives on exaggeration. For example, Hotgun favors separate statehood for Oklahoma and Indian Territory; he bases his opinion on some interesting "facts" about their respective geographical features. Fus tells us that Hotgun favors separation

> 'cause they was too much long-tailed cyclones out in Oklahoma and people was had to live right close to a hole in the ground like prairie dogs to keep out a they way. Hotgun he say he is not used to that kind of living and was get too old to learn to act like a prairie dog. Then he say sometime the people what had a hole in the ground was not out a danger, 'cause the rivers out in Oklahoma had no banks to um and was spread out all over the country when they get up, like maple syrup on a hot flapjack. (102–3)

Tookpafka Micco adds:

> Hotgun aint told half of it, 'cause out in Oklahoma they was had a drought in the summer time and hard times in the fall, 'sides blizzards in the winter time and cyclones with long tails in the spring. Tookpafka Micco was mighty bitter and he say he was druther had a sofky patch in Injin Territory than a big country full a debt and chinch bugs in Oklahoma. (103)

Hotgun and his partner paint a picture full of "tall talk," like the novels of Mark Twain, but at times they reminisce about life in their hometown of Muskogee. Putting a live coal into his pipe, Hotgun says:

> Well, so the New Year was made me lonesome for olden times put near twenty-five years ago, when you could go up to Muskogee and hear the cayotes [sic] howling in the back ground and yanking up the shoats where they was now talking about putting up a opera house long enough for fifteen hundred people to all get killed in. (152–53)

Tookpafka Micco follows his partner's leap into nostalgia: "Well, so they was lots a changes been made up to Muskogee and you couldn't hardly locate yourself you didn't had a policeman" (153). Hotgun replies, "Well, so then you could go in the shack restaurant and eat and didn't have to have a string band to whet your appetite" (153). But Tookpafka Micco has the final say: "Well, so them days the store keeper and hod carrier didn't eat dinner at supper time and jackasses didn't try to be elks" (153).

The two commentators never seem to tire of speaking about the changes in Indian Territory. Often they discuss how their friends have sold all their allotted land, making them, at least temporarily, affluent. But Hotgun and Tookpafka also worry about the consequences of such rapid change. Hotgun describes the results of two cultures clashing, transforming Indian Territory into a surreal landscape:

> So everywhere you go now you find lightning rod for clothes line and steel range cook stoves for the children's play house, and calender [sic] clocks for ornament over the fire place and Gale harrows for scrap iron and old buggies for curiosities. (168)

Hotgun and Tookpafka Micco look for a safe haven where conservative Creeks like themselves can live. They conclude that they must learn to live with the grafters and other shysters who are rooted in Indian Territory. Tookpafka tries to reassure his readers, "Well, so the Injin was had to go up against it to learn and, maybe so, after while he catch on" (165). Tookpafka Micco suggests that not only do "Injins" learn, but they learn too well the corrupt ways of the whites.

Hotgun and Tookpafka Micco survive because of their comic stance; they displace their fears into a kind of play, which temporarily relieves them, and other Indians like them, from the seriousness of their situation.

They concoct scenes in which whites, especially the powerful politicians running Indian Territory, appear stupid and ridiculous. Through their own form of storytelling, Hotgun and Tookpafka Micco transform these politicians into small and insignificant people. For instance, Hotgun enjoys retelling the story of when President Theodore Roosevelt visited Indian Territory. In his story, everyone appears ludicrous, especially the president; he is the epitome of the "white man" touring "exotic" Indian country.

Hotgun describes Roosevelt's speech, full of empty platitudes; then he tells how the president congratulates the townspeople on their "fine town." However, the president tells the Indian people: "But I didn't had time to talk any more, 'cause I couldn't stop here but two minutes and I have been here put near five. So long" (204). Hotgun parodies Roosevelt, a politician bent on meeting his people, in a calculated "minute" performance.

President Roosevelt—the most powerful and visible white man in the country—becomes a person acting out inappropriate behavior, lacking the wisdom of how to conduct himself in a social situation. Hotgun in his flagrant caricature of a "very big white man" reduces him to an ignorant, stupid person, for Roosevelt is a "big man" as president, but he is also a huge, fat white man. It is essentially playful commenting with a malicious intent. Hotgun continues with his story:

> Then the special train was kick up a cloud of dust and hide behind it, and the multitude was climb down off the houses and telegraph poles and go tell they neighbors 'bout it. Colonel Clarence B. Duglast he go and tell his friends the President think he was ten cents straight, and Chief P. Porter he go and tell his friends the President he say he was the greatest living Injin, and Charley Gibson he go and write a "Rifle Shot" 'bout giving the President a fan made out of tame turkey feathers instead of eagle plumes, and Alice M. Lobbysome she go and buy the platform the President stood on for a souvenir. Maybe so she was made a bedstead out of it and distribute the sawdust and shaving among the full-bloods to look at. (204–205)

Hotgun exposes several games going on at once. In fact, the president's stop becomes a three-ring circus. While the townspeople climb down from the telegraph poles and roof tops, "Colonel Duglast" acts like a clown-figure as he tries to decipher the president's cryptic message, which no one seems to understand. Hotgun completes his comic scenario with Creek chief Porter being deemed the most distinguished "living Indian" by the president, while Charley Gibson, the author of "Rifle Shots," presents Roosevelt with "turkey feathers" instead of eagle feathers.

With this ludicrous parodic scene, Hotgun transforms a stuffy ceremonious event into comedy, complete with an acerbic bite. Alice M. Lobbysome purchases the "platform" as a "memento," which later, like a sacred religious artifact, she distributes in its sawdust form to the full-bloods to "worship." The next stop on the presidential tour is "out in Oklahoma in a big pasture, where they was lots of cayotes" (205). Hotgun continues:

> He was got after one a horseback and crowd it over the prairies till he was get good results and captured it alive. He was had lots of fun with it before he was run it down. The President was a great hunter and was kill big game well as a cayote or jackrabbit. So he was go on to the Rocky Mountains to beard the bear and lion in they den. (205)

Tookpafka adds the final touch to the story: "Well, so this time the Lord better help the grizzly" (205). Hotgun and Tookpafka complete a perfect circle of Indian humor as they jibe at the methods and behaviors of the president. Tookpafka Micco's desire to get the Lord on the side of the grizzly bear is an exaggeration, assuming praise for Roosevelt as a big game hunter. But Hotgun and Tookpafka Micco are making fun of Roosevelt's "gross" being, the hunter, as he hunts for the "fun" of running game down. For Creeks, hunting is considered hard work, not a sport; furthermore, hunting is a community enterprise. Hotgun pokes fun at the president's tendency to be self-absorbed and his zealous desire to set himself apart from others as a great hunter. To Hotgun and Tookpafka Micco, the president's actions seem patently misguided. Roosevelt becomes a "large" target for their amusement. Whereas Hotgun and Tookpafka Micco's remarks seem innocent, slippage reveals the covertly ironic intent of their comments.

Hotgun and Tookpafka Micco's comic perspective is also built on word play. Their words are often inventive, as when Tookpafka Micco combines classical allusions with barnyard animals. Tookpafka Micco describes the voice of the South McAlester postmaster, Henry Be Robbing (Henry P. Robbins):

> He was had a fine voice with music in it like a mule braying in the meadow, and he knowed it all like a set a encyclopedia. . . . He was

> worked 'em up like Mark Anthony when Ceaser [*sic*] was died
> with his boots on. (114)

Tookpafka Micco makes a devastatingly funny comment. He confuses his classical reference as well, having Caesar, like Custer, die with his boots on.

Or Fus retells how Hotgun describes Crazy Snake after the federal authorities put him in prison: "Hotgun he say they was shaved [Crazy Snake's] head like it was some mule's tail" (73). But this allusion does not mean to be funny in the same manner as the Henry Be Robbing example. Here, we note Crazy Snake, a revered Creek leader, being shorn like an animal. Posey's down-home witticism reveals the bitter irony of white domination.

Hotgun and Tookpafka Micco use down-home sayings, but their words mediate between two worlds, Indian and white. They also refer to "side shows," perhaps alluding to Buffalo Bill's Wild West Show, a popular entertainment that millions of people in the United States and Canada, as well as in Europe, attended, witnessing the "spectacular" performance of "wild" Indians on horseback. In one incident, Tookpafka Micco compares Indian Territory politics to a side show. He tells Hotgun, "Well, maybe so the side show was start up now pretty soon with variations and the people was had a chance to say it was a fake and want they money back" (148).

In another incident Hotgun equates the politics of Crazy Snake with the image of Bosco, a "geek" known for his feat of eating live snakes. He refers to Crazy Snake's die-hard politics: "[Crazy Snake] wouldn't give it up for a circus with three rings in it and the band playing 'Hiawatha' and the ticket man hollering, 'Well so you was had to hurry if you see Bosco eat the copperhead alive!'" (144). This conflation of images, Bosco the geek with Crazy Snake, reveals a morbid perspective. Yet the circus and its freaky sideshows appropriately describe some of the events transpiring in Indian Territory.

Hotgun and Tookpafka Micco cut a window into their Creek world by creating comic play. Sometimes these two tease meisters simply conflate dissimilar images as their own form of verbal wit. Like the people standing in awe while Bosco swallows live snakes, they gape at Euroamerican politics, helping their readers cope with the conscious, brutal world of grafters and pompous politicians. Most often, their humor bites at reality. It is, as Paula Gunn Allen comments, a kind of bitter humor "because it's so close to the bone" (Coltelli, 22).

What makes this humor so powerful is that it mirrors life in Indian Territory. It is a way of expressing frustrations and hostilities. As Allen's comment suggests, Hotgun and Tookpafka Micco laugh to survive; they make jokes to renew themselves and others; their comic vision is to overcome erasure, denial, invisibility, and annihilation. They create humor to encircle and to contain the humiliation and the bitterness that being an Indian encompasses. Humor, as Lincoln suggests, "refuses to give in to the pain; it administers an aesthetic to make pain the very subject of its pleasure" (55).

Hotgun and Tookpafka Micco administer comic medicine that helps others stomach bicultural dissonance. Tookpafka Micco reflects, smoking slowly as he carefully chooses his words: "Well so the Lord helps 'em that help 'emselves—except the Injun" (Littlefield and Hunter, *Fus*, 243). Hotgun and Tookpafka Micco "home in" to the reality of trying to occupy a shifting space. They prescribe laughter that rips apart politicians' tactics, turns white heroes into fearless "cayotes" and jackrabbits. Their humor transforms political "platforms" into false religious icons.

Hotgun and Tookpafka Micco's comic stance enables them to overcome a shifting political and economical world. Hotgun proclaims: "The Injin is civilized and aint extinct no more than a rabbit. He's just beginning to feel his breakfast food" (217). As Deloria comments, "When a people can laugh at themselves and laugh at others and hold all aspects of life together without letting anybody drive them to extremes, then it seems to me that people can survive" (167).

7

COMING FULL CIRCLE
ALEX POSEY AND AMERICAN LITERATURE

*I look for evidence of other Creeks, for remnants of voices,
or for tobacco brown bones to come wandering
down Conti Street, Royale, or Decatur.*
                              —*Creek poet Joy Harjo*[1]

Posey left the image that he had so desired in the photograph that remains
by the side of my desk where I work. His stylish hat, cocked to the side,
makes him look undaunted as he stares demurely off to the side, refusing
to face the photographer. Yet his photograph reflects the enigmatic nature
of his life work; he poses, assuming the stance that Robert Burns or other
well-known nineteenth-century poets make for a photographer who wants
the appearance of portentousness. This possibility seems plausible as I
peer deep into Posey's face, looking for clues to understand him. Would
Posey want to be placed alongside Burns or next to Henry David Thoreau,
or would he be pleased to have this photographic portrait beside that of
his Creek journalist friend Charles Gibson? Is the solution simply to
uncover another photograph that reveals the many faceted aspects of his
life? I sense, however, that Posey chose his stance for a specific reason: he
wanted to be "seen" like a Euroamerican poet, and that is how whites in
the nineteenth century most likely envisioned him. He struck a stance like
Burns, but his image inadvertently signifies his conflictedness and that of
his work. Posey thus is not a facile literary figure one easily "sees" and
"reads," though he leaves traces of himself in his photographic and verbal
images.

To trace Posey's beliefs about Indian identity and culture one must look
at his use of narrative strategies that often contradict and sometimes col-
lide with one another; the power of his work resides in the apparent con-
tradictions and collisions. Posey, as we have seen, finds it difficult to render
a metaphysical experience within the strict definitions of Western poetry.
He tries to break out, as the pig wants to wander away from Uncle Dick's

pen in "Uncle Dick's Sow" or as the speaker "breaks out" of the four walls in "Tulledega." In contrast to his Fus Fixico letters, his short stories, and other Creek verbal writings, his poetry seems stilted and lacking in artistic expression; his words fall short, revealing the personal and cultural tension of trying to maintain two worldviews. It is only in a few exceptional poems, such as "Tulledega", "An Outcast," or "Hotgun on the Death of Yadeka Harjo," that Posey severs himself from the use of sentimental language and shows his readers a glimpse of his efforts to mediate Indian and white world-views. It is not clear why this slippage is more apparent in his poetry than in the other genres in which he wrote, except that Posey had stopped writing poetry early in his literary career and had reevaluated his writing. He also appears to have been defensive toward his poetry, explaining that "I write entirely for my own pleasure and am entirely indifferent to reward or criticism" (Littlefield, *Posey,* 119). Perhaps Posey sensed his own inadequacies at this stage of his career, as well as his difficulty in mastering the poetic form.

Nevertheless, it is evident that in the majority of his poetry he wishes to erase his Indianness, and instead emulates the supposed "loftily height" of verse, similar to Burns. When Posey does listen to his own sensibilities as a poet, he modifies the Western poetry model by allowing his Indian character, Hotgun, to speak "Indian," commenting on what it means to be an Indian. Hotgun's remarks are poignant and riveting as Posey reveals the paradoxical position of his own Indian character.

We have looked at Posey's difficulty in negotiating texts. His attempt to erase his own Indian identity leads him sometimes to slip into conventional Western modes of writing, particularly in much of his poetry. But the truth is that the problem of cultural differentiation influences all of his work—even surfacing in his most conventional writing, his poetry. It is something that Posey cannot contain; it seeps out of the edges of his poetry and of his own Westernized photograph. Paula Gunn Allen writes about the difficulty of participating in two cultures: "A contemporary American Indian is always faced with a dual perception of the world: that which is particular to American Indian life and that which exists ignorant of that life" (41). It is this convergence of two cultural codes, an attempt to balance, then bring together, divergent worldviews, that shapes Posey's writing and connects him with other nineteenth-century Indian writers such as Charles Gibson and Ora Eddleman Reed and with contemporary Native American writers.

Posey struggled to find his voice in Western poetry, and he was largely unsuccessful. But in writing Creek verbal stories, he found his own artistic expression in storytelling. He situates his short stories "Mose and Richard" and "Uncle Dick's Sow" within the borders of Indian Territory, focusing on local characters such as Mose and Richard, two young Creek blacks, who spend their time dodging their school lessons, and Uncle Dick, a Creek freedman farmer and his runaway pig. Like Mark Twain and Bret Harte, Posey situates his characters within the unsettled and unpopulated regions of the western territories. Posey's Uncle Dick and his rebellious pig resemble Jim Smiley and his jumping frog in Twain's "The Celebrated Jumping Frog of Calaveras County." Whereas Twain uses a storytelling frame in his short story to comment on the difference between western and eastern worldviews, Posey's Uncle Dick uncovers the cultural and racial biases of Indians, blacks, and whites as they collide on the Indian landscape in Indian Territory.

Like Twain and Harte, Posey uses dialect to ground his characters in their rural surroundings; Mose and Richard converse in black English and Uncle Dick speaks Creek English, while the pig becomes the most proficient linguist, speaking standard English, Creek, and black English.[2] Most important, "Uncle Dick's Sow" converts a trickster-like tale into literary satire that interrogates the positions of white, Indian, and black subjectivities. His story reveals shifting identities: pigs, Indians, blacks, and whites collide and change alliances, thus offering an inherent conflict over the position of Indian.

Posey's short stories fit within the genre of "local color" or "regional" fiction, characteristic of post-Civil War writers, including Bret Harte, Mark Twain, Alice Brown, George Washington Cable, Sarah Orne Jewett, Kate Chopin, Mary E. Wilkins Freeman, Charles Chesnutt, and other, equally important American fiction writers. Among this group of writers, Chesnutt, Sui Sin Far, Zitkala-Ša, and Alice Dunbar-Nelson represent the few minority writers of the late-nineteenth-century who appear in national publications. Zitkala-Ša, a Sioux writer, who published "Impressions of an Indian Childhood" in the January 1900 edition of *Atlantic Monthly,* is the only American Indian who is included with local colorists or regional writers. While Zitkala-Ša, Jewett, Freeman, Chopin, Harte, and Hamlin Garland, as well as other writers, contributed their work to *Atlantic Monthly* and other eastern magazines, Posey published his short stories in territorial publications such as *Twin Territories* or the *Indian Journal.* Yet being called a local colorist certainly did not tarnish the reputation of Harte or Twain as it seems to have relegated Jewett, Freeman, Chopin, Sui Sin Far, Chesnutt, and Zitkala-Ša to the margins of American fiction. For these fiction writers, *local colorist* became a diminishing term. They were also held down by their gender and ethnicity, unlike the white male local colorists. Posey seems to have internalized his position as a minor writer, believing that his work would not appeal to a national audience, since his writings merely addressed local people and their circumstances (Littlefield, *Posey*, 118). In contrast to the work of Jewett, Freeman, or Zitkala-Ša, Posey's short stories reached only a relatively small readership; even though *Twin Territories* circulated in the Midwest and East, its subscription was insignificant compared to *Atlantic Monthly*'s. Nevertheless, Posey's short-story writings have much in common with local colorists and regionalist writers of the late-nineteenth-century; but his writings, including his Fus Fixico letters, which were published in national newspapers, have only recently been introduced to the nineteenth-century American literary tradition.[3]

Throughout his life, Posey remained fascinated with the people and the landscape of Indian Territory, and he continued writing and listening to stories that he had heard from various Indian storytellers. His stories "Chinnubbie and the Owl" and "The 'Possum and the Skunk" are in touch with a tradition originating from a distant past. He sensed their importance as a way to understand the beliefs and verbal traditions of his Creek ancestors, for all these stories reveal important insights about human motivations and behaviors. For instance, Opossum bragging to Skunk about his big bushy tail mirrors human experiences and relationships and instructs listeners as to how they should behave in similar circumstances. The story warns about the dangers of being too pompous, a trait that transgresses group solidarity. For all of his leanings toward verbal tradition, Posey obviously understood and valued the profound meaning of these tales. His stories focus on how animals and people relate and create meaning out of their world, and in his listening to these stories, Posey recognized the transformational qualities that the audience must undergo when listening to such stories. Paula Gunn Allen calls such stories "magic: it is the area of relationship between all those parts of experience that commonly divide us from ourselves, our universe, and our fellows" (*The Sacred Hoop*, 117).

Like the writings of many other Indian authors, Posey's work comes alive in his writings of Creek literature, where there are "no monkeys with their tails stamped off calling themselves people, [and] all the animals talked together" ("The 'Possum and the Skunk"). His stories recreate a mythical time that emanates from a traditional Indian point of view. In "Chinnubbie and the Owl," Chinnubbie departs in the "twilight of the blossoming day, like a dream on his journey to search to—he knew not where," but we imagine that he goes away to bring back another story. Like his persona Chinnubbie, Posey cherished storytelling, and he spent a large part of his life searching his own neck of the woods for Creek stories, which he preserved for many other generations to read and appreciate.

Posey's Fus Fixico letters have their roots, as with his Creek stories, in Creek verbal tradition. Like the Creek stories, the Fus Fixico letters represent the talk of a community of full-blooded Creeks. Their conversations mimic the way tribal affairs are talked about and discussed among people, with no one person dominating the entire discussion. Instead, Fus "repeats" Hotgun and Tookpafka Micco, along with the conversations of Wolf Warrior and Kono Harjo. All participate, to some degree, in the "talk" in an effort to work out meaning about the problems going on in Indian Territory. There is no single distinctive, authorial voice that speaks, but multiple voices participate in the discussions. It is this collective of voices that mirrors the verbal tradition that Posey renders so well. Not only did he recreate the performative aspect of Creek verbal traditions but he found an effective method to critique the political circumstances of Indian Territory, enabling his full-blooded characters to deride and ridicule the nefarious dealings of white politicians and federal officials as they legislated laws that overruled tribal governments, eroding their close-knit community atmosphere.

Simon Ortiz asserts that the colonial experience drives much of Native American literature—it is the springboard that writers react against as they try to discover meaning in their own lives, redefining their Indian identities and community experiences. Thus "white" encounters leave their traces in verbal literature; these tales recount white men usurping Indian lands or white invaders bearing whiskey and Euroamerican diseases—things that initially destroyed many Indian populations and drastically altered tribal life. Other stories explain how Euroamerican domination comes into play. In one Creek story, a dead Creek chief speaks to Gohantone, the current chief:

> This land belongs to you and your children forever. This land
> will be yours forever, but these whites who have just come will

overwhelm you and inherit your land. They will increase and the
Indian will decrease and at last die out. Then only white people
will remain. But there will be terrible times. (Lankford, 137)

Creek tales, like many other tribal stories, recount what happens to all
Native peoples who have suffered from imperialism and colonization. The
struggle to maintain cultural integrity is exemplified by Posey's Hotgun
and his friends as they talk about the maneuverings of white and Indian
politicians and land grafters. They illustrate a condition common to all
Native peoples. Their talk is the talk of all tribal peoples struggling to
survive Euroamerican domination.

Many critics have willingly introduced contemporary Indian writing to
the American literature canon, but they have forged ahead without under-
standing its origins and multiple functions. Much of what we ascribe to
this literature is often rooted in a restrictive literary context, therefore lim-
iting our understanding and thus, of course, our appreciation of textual
representation, structures, and strategies. The narrative strategies of Charles
Chesnutt or Posey, for example, demonstrate that in their writings both
authors address multiple audiences, and as a consequence, their texts
appear to reveal complicit intentionalities. Furthermore, as we have seen,
Posey adapts verbal traditions to his prose. Literary devices, such as his
use of trickster-like strategies, need to be investigated in order to under-
stand writers who draw from bicultural experiences as well as to help read-
ers see the connections between literature and culture. The current trend
to incorporate American Indian works into the canon should include
works by early-nineteenth-century Native American writers such as Posey,
who wrote about the impact of colonialism on his people, developed a dis-
tinctive literary style while writing in several genres, and created texts that
speak of cultural difference. Posey's work also reveals the struggle for the
production of Native American literature that may challenge current views
about how we now regard Indian literature.

Paula Gunn Allen refers to writers, like Posey, whose voices have been
silenced, cut off, severed from the mainstream literary tradition. She says,
"We are the people who have no shape or form, whose invisibility is not
visual only but of the voice as well; we speak but we are not heard" (35).
One could suggest that a culture and its literature can be understood best
if one listens to the multiple voices that have been covered up for so many
years. Posey's work shows us the way out of a limited literary perspective,

opening up a new and perhaps a more thorough understanding of American Indian literature. Alex Posey, silenced for almost one hundred years, helps us circle back to the roots of contemporary American Indian literature, giving critics and readers a different basis for understanding the difficulty of negotiating, and ultimately expressing, bicultural experiences.

NOTES

CHAPTER 1

1. This is an excerpt from Posey's Fus Fixico letter [no. 44], in which Hotgun is critiquing the dramatic changes in Indian Territory as a result of the "grafter" entrance into Indian lands. See Littlefield and Hunter, *Fus Fixico Letters*, 167, for a full account of this particular letter.

2. These five nations are referred to as the Five Civilized Tribes. This term draws attention to the five nations' rapid assimilation to Euroamerican culture, as compared to that by other tribal peoples. However, I do not particularly like this term. It seems to me that "Five Civilized Tribes" simply reifies the dichotomous position of the colonizer/colonist, savage/civilized. Instead, I prefer to use "five southeastern nations" or the "five nations" to refer collectively to the Creek, Choctaw, Seminole, Cherokee, and Chickasaw peoples.

3. For a detailed overview of the five nations' migration and assimilation into Indian Territory, see Foreman, *The Five Civilized Tribes*, and Debo, *And Still the Waters Run*.

4. See Debo, *And Still the Waters Run*, 67–70, for more detailed information regarding Indian schools in Indian Territory.

5. Debo, *And Still the Waters Run*, 8, states that the Choctaws and Creeks tried to publish a tribal newspaper, but they were not as successful as the Cherokees. For more information about the various Indian-owned newspapers, see Foreman, *Oklahoma Imprints*. Also, *Twin Territories* was owned for several years by Ora Eddleman Reed, a Cherokee editor and writer. Her paper featured Indian fiction writers and other Indian-related topics. For more information on this publication, see Witcher, "Territorial Magazines," 484–97, or Littlefield and Parins, *American Indian and Alaska Native Newspapers and Periodicals*, 566–69.

6. The article that appeared in the *New York Times* was called "The Indian Daily Journal"; in the summer of 1903 *The Indian Journal* became a daily publication.

7. See Littlefield and Hunter, introduction to *The Fus Fixico Letters*, 19, for an account of the extent of the publication of the Fus Fixico letters in national, Canadian, and British newspapers.

CHAPTER 2

1. This story, collected by E. A. Hitchcock, who visited the Creeks in 1842, stresses the Indians' inability to read "white paper" as something that sets them apart and limits their possibilities. To some extent, this story alludes to "white paper" as having a magical presence, something that Euroamericans are invested with and that Indians have not acquired. "The Power of the Word" is found in Lankford, ed., *Native America Legends*, 139. The story's underlying assumption suggests that illiteracy keeps Native people shackled to white domination.

2. Asbury mission, an Indian boarding school founded and run by the Methodists, was located near North Fork Town, a settlement situated between the Canadian and North Fork Rivers in Oklahoma. For more history about this mission, see Foreman, *The Five Civilized Tribes*, 196–97.

3. According to Debo, full-bloods were allowed to sell only eighty acres of their allotment. See *And Still the Waters Run*, 89–91, for more information regarding the complicated governmental restrictions levied on land allotments.

4. See Littlefield, *Posey*, 172–73, for further information concerning the election for the chief's office.

5. Charles Gibson, along with other candidates, ran for position of the Creek principal chief. Posey enthusiastically endorsed his old friend, but Gibson withdrew from the race in July 1903. Perhaps that is why Gibson cannot fire his rifle: he is too disappointed at his own poor performance in the election.

6. Little scholarly work has been done on "Red English." Yet an interesting text translated into Red English is *The Golden Woman: The Colville Narrative of Peter J. Seymour*, ed. Mattina. In his introduction, Mattina states that he believes Red English is a "pan-Indian phenomenon" having various dialectic variations. He also points out the reluctance of many edi-

tors to publish his text because of their belief that Red English is inferior to standard English. Although he makes no value judgments about Red English's grammar or usage, he believes that many non-Indians have perpetuated negative stereotypes about the "semi-articulate or primitive or backward Indians" (9). Mattina states that "rather than changing the way Indians talk, I advocate educating those who hear Indians talk" (9).

7. *Twin Territories* was published from 1898 until 1904. See Littlefield and Parins, *American Indian and Alaska Native Newspapers and Periodicals*, 566–69, and Foreman, *Oklahoma Imprints*, 237–39.

8. The cover was changed for the October 1902 issue.

CHAPTER 3

1. This is an excerpt from a letter written by Alex Posey, which can be found in *The Poems of Alexander Lawrence Posey*, comp. Minnie Posey. Unless otherwise indicated, the poems quoted in this chapter have also been taken from this work.

2. This poem is quoted from Alexander Posey's handwritten notes in the Alexander Posey Collection, located at the Thomas Gilcrease Institute of American History and Art, Tulsa, Okla. The poem varies slightly from the version found in *Poems of Alexander Posey*, comp. M. Posey.

3. This poem is quoted also from Alexander Posey's handwritten notes in the Posey Collection. It varies slightly from the version found in *Poems of Alexander Posey*, comp. M. Posey.

4. Although a small point in the context of the larger discussion, Thoreau's complete glossing over of the Indian's reference to the "the deer that went a shopping" points out an important cultural difference between Thoreau and Posey. Thoreau never even acknowledges the humorous reference of his informant. I am certain that Posey, however, would have appreciated this comment. We will see later that Posey had a keen sense of humor, as revealed in his poem "Hotgun on the Death of Yadeka Harjo."

5. Posey's poem "The Indian's Past Olympic" appears to be derived from watching modern Creek ball games. Littlefield mentions an especially spectacular ball game between two towns (Arbekas and Eufaula) in the fall of 1905, which Posey claims was "the bloodiest game ever pulled off in Indian Territory" (Littlefield, *Posey*, 201).

6. Swanton uses the Spanish spelling of the **word:** *caseena.* It is listed in

A World Guide to Lesser-Known Edible Plants as *caseena* or *dahoon holly*, a tea substitute made from the dried leaves that yield the beverage after being boiled in water.

7. See Peterson, "An Indian, an American: Ethnicity, Assimilation and Balance in Charles Eastman's *From the Deep Woods to Civilization*," as a prime example of another Native American writer who deals with assimilating into Euroamerican society.

CHAPTER 4

1. This excerpt is taken from a clipping from the Bacone newspaper, dated approximately between 1889 and 1895. This is part of the Posey Collection #4126.

2. William E. Connelley, who wrote the introduction to *The Poems of Alexander Posey*, comp. M. Posey, stated that "Chinnubbie" originally was derived from Creek mythology, which Posey changed considerably. Connelley states that Chinnubbie had been a supernatural hero endowed with some human traits; Posey, according to Connelley, transformed Chinnubbie into the "evil genius of the Creeks." However, after investigating various ethnographic sources and other collections of Southeastern Native American folktales, such as Swanton, *Myths and Tales of the Southeastern Indians*, Mooney, *Myths of the Cherokee*, and J. and A. Kilpatrick, *Friends of Thunder*, it is evident that Connelley is mistaken. Chinnubbie is not a traditional Creek trickster figure that Posey reshaped to fit his own literary taste, but is indeed Posey's own literary invention. According to Littlefield, it is likely that Posey heard trickster tales from his mother and reinvented Chinnubbie as his persona. It is probable, as Littlefield believes, that the name Chinnubbie also could have been one of his mother's story characters.

3. Rabbit as a trickster figure is pervasive and found throughout the Southeast. Similar stories about Rabbit's adventures can be found in Cherokee, Chickasaw, Choctaw, and Seminole tribal lore. See J. and A. Kilpatrick, *Friends of Thunder*, for examples of Cherokee rabbit tales or ethnographic material already mentioned. Furthermore, it should be noted that Rabbit appears as Brer Rabbit, a familiar figure in African-American stories. There is much debate about the origins of African-American tales, which dates back to the publication in 1880 of Joel Chandler Harris's *Uncle Remus: His Songs and Sayings*, as to whether African-American tales

were of European, African, or Native American origin. For an overview concerning this debate, see Florence Baer, introduction to *Sources and Analogues of the Uncle Remus Tales*. Also, Zumwalt, ed., *American Folklore Scholarship*, 130–35, provides a similar synopsis concerning the debate over origins of the trickster Rabbit.

4. This particular newspaper clipping is from the Bacone newspaper, dated approximately between 1889 and 1894, and can be found in the Posey Collection #74.

5. There is an enormous overlapping in Posey's rendering of black and Creek dialect; in fact, it is difficult to distinguish the two except when he uses Creek words to differentiate Creek from black dialect. It seems to me an examination of Posey's use of dialect alongside the use of dialect by other writers such as Cooper and Twain would be an important site for investigation for those trained in linguistics. Such an investigation falls beyond the scope of this particular study.

CHAPTER 5

1. From the poem "Wagon Full of Thunder," in *Harper's Anthology of Twentieth Century Native American Poetry*, ed. Niatum, 5.

2. Both of these stories are found in Swanton, *Myths*. An interesting addition to the first story is also found in J. and A. Kilpatrick, eds., *Friends of Thunder*. The snake, sometimes referred to as the Horned Serpent, is the Uk'ten in the Cherokee verbal tradition. Anna Kilpatrick interviews two Cherokee storytellers, Asudi and Yan'sa, about their beliefs regarding the Uk'ten. The text also includes numerous Uk'ten stories.

3. "Fable of the Foolish Young Bear" appeared in the *Indian Journal*, March 22, 1901; "A Creek Fable" appeared in *Twin Territories*, October 1900.

4. Oliver recounts a detailed account of the Creek cosmos in *Chasers of the Sun*.

5. The Creeks, Choctaws, Seminoles, and Chickasaws share similar verbal traditions. Many stories are found in the story traditions of all of these cultures.

6. Posey's version of the tale is similar to the Cherokee version called "Why the Possum's Tail Is Bare." See Mooney, *Myths of the Cherokee*, 269. Another version, "Why the Opossum Has No Hair," although not as similar to the one Posey relates, can be found in Swanton, *Myths*, 41.

CHAPTER 6

1. "Trickster" in *In Mad Love and War,* by Joy Harjo (Middletown: Wesleyan University Press, 1990).

2. Posey published seventy-two Fus Fixico letters. In 1902, he bought the *Eufaula Indian Journal,* a weekly newspaper, in which he published his first letters. When he sold the *Indian Journal* in 1903, his letters appeared in the *Fort Smith Times;* in 1904, he left the *Times,* and his letters appeared in the *Muskogee Phoenix.* In 1904, he became a fieldworker for the Dawes Commission, and he failed to publish on a regular basis until he resumed the editorship of the *Indian Journal,* just prior to his death in 1908. For a more detailed biographic sketch of Posey's publishing career, see Littlefield, *Posey.*

3. It should be noted that Posey was probably influenced by journalist Finley Peter Dunne's prototype Mr. Dooley, an Irish bartender, who espouses his poignant but humorous opinions about American politics. Mr. Dooley has a confidante, Mr. Hennessy, who listens to his friend's comments. See Littlefield and Hunter, introduction to *Fus Fixico Letters,* for an overview of Posey's journalistic influences. See also Eckely, *Finley Peter Dunne,* 22–35, for a brief sketch about the origins of Mr. Dooley.

4. This is translated as "Blow in it for him." Littlefield explains that in making medicine, a person blows through a small cane with a hole in it into the bucket of medicine.

5. According to Littlefield, both Wolf Warrior and Kono Harjo are fictional characters. See Littlefield and Hunter, introduction to *Fus Fixico Letters,* 35, for more information concerning the creation of Wolf Warrior and Kono Harjo.

6. Littlefield notes that this is a favorite Creek corn dish. He describes it as like grits, but seasoned with grease and salt and cooked with wild game.

CHAPTER 7

1. From the poem "New Orleans," in Harjo, *She Had Some Horses.*

2. For a discussion of Creek and black dialect, see Littlefield, "Short Fiction Writers of the Indian Territory," 28–31.

3. Lauter, ed., *Heath Anthology of American Literature,* Vol. 2, includes Posey's "Ode to Sequoyah" and "Hotgun on the Death of Yadeka Harjo"

and one of his Fus Fixico letters (no. 44) in its collection of American literature. Furthermore, Littlefield and Hunter have published all of Posey's Fus Fixico letters in *Fus Fixico Letters*.

BIBLIOGRAPHY

Allen, Paula Gunn. "Answering the Deer: Genocide and Continuance in American Indian Women's Poetry." *American Indian Culture and Research Journal* 6 (1982): 35–45.

———. *The Sacred Hoop*. Boston: Beacon Press, 1986.

Ashcroft, Bill, Gareth Griffiths, and Helen Tiffin. *The Empire Writes Back*. London and New York: Routledge Press, 1989.

Babcock, Barbara A. "The Story in the Story: Metanarration in Folk Narrative." In *Verbal Art as Performance,* by Richard Bauman. Rowley, Mass.: Newbury House, 1977.

Baer, Florence. *Sources and Analogues of the Uncle Remus Tales*. Helsinki: Suomalainen Tiedeakatemia, 1980.

Barnett, Leona G. "Este Charte Emunkv." *Chronicles of Oklahoma* 46 (1968–69): 20–40.

Basso, Keith H. *Portraits of the 'Whiteman': Linguistic Play and Cultural Symbols among the Western Apache*. Cambridge: Cambridge University Press, 1979.

Bauman, Richard. *Story, Performance, and Event*. Cambridge and New York: Cambridge University Press, 1986.

———. *Verbal Art as Performance*. Rowley, Mass.: Newbury House, 1977.

Bauman, Richard, and Charles L. Briggs. "Poetics and Performance as Critical Perspectives on Language and Social Life." *Annual Review of Anthropology* 19 (1990): 59–88.

Briggs, Charles L. *Competence in Performance: The Creativity of Tradition in Mexicano Verbal Art*. Philadelphia: University of Pennsylvania Press, 1988.

Bruchac, Joseph, ed. *Survival This Way: Interviews with American Indian Poets*. Tucson: University of Arizona Press, 1987.

Challacombe, Doris. "Alexander Lawrence Posey." *Chronicles of Oklahoma* 11 (1933): 1011–18.

Coltelli, Laura, ed. *Winged Words: American Indian Writers Speak*. Lincoln: University of Nebraska Press, 1990.

Dale, Edward Everett. "The Journal of Alexander Lawrence Posey." *Chronicles of Oklahoma* 45 (1967–68): 398–432.

Debo, Angie. *And Still the Waters Run*. Princeton: Princeton University Press, 1991.

Deloria, Vine. *Custer Died for Your Sins: An Indian Manifesto*. London: MacMillian Company, 1969.

Dippie, Brian W. *The Vanishing Indian*. Middletown: Wesleyan University Press, 1982.

Eastman, Charles A. *From the Deep Woods to Civilization: Chapters in the Autobiography of an Indian*. 1916. Reprint, Lincoln: University of Nebraska Press, 1977.

———. *Indian Boyhood*. 1902. Reprint, Greenwich, Conn.: Fawcett, 1977.

Eckley, Grace. *Finley Peter Dunne*. Boston: Twayne, 1981.

Eddleman Reed, Ora V. "What the Curious Want to Know." *Muskogee (Creek Nation) Twin Territories,* February 1901.
———. "What the Curious Want To Know." *Muskogee (Creek Nation) Twin Territories,* April 1901.
Eufaula (Okla.) Indian Journal, May 1, 1990.
Finnegan, Ruth. *Oral Traditions and the Verbal Arts.* London and New York: Routledge Press, 1992.
Foreman, Carolyn Thomas. *Oklahoma Imprints, 1835–1907.* Norman: University of Oklahoma Press, 1936.
Foreman, Grant. *The Five Civilized Tribes.* Norman: University of Oklahoma Press, 1989.
Freud, Sigmund. *Jokes and Their Relation to the Unconscious.* Translated and edited by James Strachey. London: 1905. Reprint, Hogarth Press, 1960.
Fussell, Edwin. *Frontier: American Literature and the American West.* Princeton: Princeton University Press, 1965.
Gibson, Charles. "'The Is-Spo-Ko-Kee Creek." *Muskogee (Creek Nation) Twin Territories,* March 1901.
———. "Rifle Shots." *Eufaula (Creek Nation) Indian Journal,* May 1, 1900.
———. "Rifle Shots." *Eufaula (Creek Nation) Indian Journal,* July 25, 1902.
———. "Rifle Shots." *Eufaula (Okla.) Indian Journal,* June 5, 1908.
Green, Donald E. *The Creek People.* Phoenix: Indian Tribal Series, 1973.
Green, Michael. *The Creeks.* New York: Chelsea House Publisher, 1990.
Grinde, Donald, and Quintard Taylor. "Red vs. Black: Conflict and Accommodation in the Post Civil War Indian Territory, 1867–1907." *American Indian Quarterly* 8 (1984): 211–29.
Harjo, Joy. *She Had Some Horses.* New York: Thunder's Mouth Press, 1983.
Hymes, D. H. *"In Vain I Tried to Tell You": Essays in Native American Ethnopoetics.* Philadelphia: University of Pennsylvania Press, 1981.
"The Indian Daily Journal." *New York Times,* September 1, 1903.
Kilpatrick, Jack F., and Anna G. Kilpatrick. *Friends of Thunder.* Dallas: Southern Methodist University Press, 1964.
Krupat, Arnold. *The Voice in the Margin.* Berkeley: University of California Press, 1989.
Lankford, George E., ed. *Native American Legends.* Little Rock: August House, 1987.
Lauter, Paul, ed. *The Heath Anthology of American Literature.* 2d ed. Vol. 2. Lexington, Mass.: D. C. Heath and Company, 1994.
Lincoln, Kenneth. *Indi'n Humor.* New York: Oxford University Press, 1993.
Littlefield, Daniel F. *Alex Posey: Creek Poet, Journalist, and Humorist.* Lincoln: University of Nebraska Press, 1992.
———. "Evolution of Alex Posey's Fus Fixico Persona." *Studies in American Indian Literature* 4 (1992): 136–44.
Littlefield, Daniel F., and Carol Petty Hunter, eds. *The Fus Fixico Letters.* Lincoln: University of Nebraska Press, 1993.
Littlefield, Daniel F., and James Parins. *American Indian and Alaska Native Newspapers and Periodicals, 1826–1924.* Westport, Conn.: Greenwood Press, 1984–86.
———. "Short Fiction Writers of the Indian Territory." *American Studies* 21–23 (1980–82): 23–38.
Marable, Mary, and Elaine Boylan. *A Handbook of Oklahoma Writers.* Norman: University of Oklahoma Press, 1939.
Martin, Joel W. *The Sacred Revolt.* Boston: Beacon Press, 1991.

Mattina, Anthony, ed. *The Golden Woman: The Colville Narrative of Peter J. Seymour.* Tucson: University of Arizona Press, 1985.

McGuirk, Carol. "Scottish Hero, Scottish Victim: Myths of Robert Burns." In *The History of Scottish Literature,* edited by Andrew Hook. Vol. 11. Aberdeen: Aberdeen University Press, 1987.

Mooney, James. "The Cherokee Ball Play." *The American Anthropologist* 3 (1890): 105–34.

———. *Myths of the Cherokees.* 19th Annual Report of the Bureau of American Ethnology, Pt. 1. Washington, D.C., 1897–98. 1–576.

Morrison, Daryl. "*Twin Territories*: The Indian Magazine and Its Editor, Ora Eddleman Reed." *Chronicles of Oklahoma* 60 (1982–83): 136–66.

Muskogee (Creek Nation) Twin Territories, July 1903.

Niatum, Duane, ed. *Harper's Anthology of Twentieth Century Native American Poetry.* San Francisco: HarperCollins Publishers, 1988.

Oliver, Louis Littlecoon. *Chasers of the Sun: Creek Indian Thoughts.* Greenfield Center, N.Y.: Greenfield Review Press, 1990.

Pearce, Roy Harvey. *Savagism and Civilization: A Study of the Indian and the American Mind.* Baltimore: Johns Hopkins University Press, 1953.

Peterson, Erik. "An Indian, an American: Ethnicity, Assimilation and Balance in Charles Eastman's *From the Deep Woods to Civilization.*" *Studies in American Indian Literature* 4 (summer-fall 1992): 145–60.

Posey, Alexander. "Chinnubbie and the Owl." MS scrapbook. Alexander L. Posey Collection. Thomas Gilcrease Institute of American History and Art, Tulsa, Okla.

———. Clippings from Bacone newspaper. Alexander L. Posey Collection. #4126. Thomas Gilcrease Institute of American History and Art, Tulsa, Okla.

———. "Mose and Richard." *Muskogee (Creek Nation) Twin Territories,* November 1900.

———. "Notes Afield." Alexander L. Posey Collection. Thomas Gilcrease Institute of American History and Art, Tulsa, Okla.

———. "The 'Possum and the Skunk." MS scrapbook. Alexander L. Posey Collection. Thomas Gilcrease Institute of American History and Art, Tulsa, Okla.

———. "Uncle Dick's Sow." *Muskogee (Creek Nation) Twin Territories,* January 1900.

Posey, Minnie H., comp. *The Poems of Alexander Lawrence Posey.* 1910. Reprint, revised by Okmulgee Cultural Foundation, Muskogee, Okla.: Hoffman Printing Company, 1969.

Rothenberg, J. and D., eds. *Symposium of the Whole: A Range of Discourse toward an Ethnopoetics.* Berkeley: University of California Press, 1983.

Ruppert, James. "Mediation and the Multiple Narrative in Contemporary Native American Fiction." *Texas Studies in Literature* 28 (1986): 209–25.

Sampson, David. "Robert Burns's Use of Scots Verse-Epistle Form." *Modern Language Review* 80 (1985): 17–37.

Sayre, Robert F. *Thoreau and the American Indian.* Princeton: Princeton University Press, 1977.

Silko, Leslie Marmon. "Language and Literature from a Pueblo Indian Perspective." In *English Literature: Opening Up the Canon,* edited by Leslie Fielder. Baltimore: Johns Hopkins University Press, 1981.

Smith, Henry Nash. *Virgin Land: The American West as Symbol and Myth.* Cambridge: Harvard University Press, 1970.

Strickland, Rennard. *The Indians in Oklahoma.* Norman: University of Oklahoma Press, 1989.

Swanton, John R. *Indians of the Southeastern United States*. Bureau of American Ethnology Bulletin 137. Washington, D.C., 1946. 1–943.

———. *Myths and Tales of the Southeastern Indians*. Bureau of American Ethnology Bulletin 88. Washington, D.C., 1929. 1–86.

———. *Religious Beliefs and Medical Practices of the Creek Indians*. 42d Annual Report of the Bureau of American Ethnology. Washington, D.C., 1924–25. 473–672.

Tedlock, Dennis. *Finding the Center: Narrative Poetry of the Zuni Indians*. New York: Dial Press, 1972.

Thoreau, Henry David. *The Journal of Henry David Thoreau*. Edited by Torrey Bradford and Francis H. Allen. Vols. 1–15. New York: Dover Publications, 1962.

———. *The Maine Woods*. Princeton: Princeton University Press, 1972.

———. *Walden*. New York: Bramhall House, 1951.

Whitman, Walt. *Complete Poetry and Selected Prose*. Edited, with an introduction, by James E. Miller Jr. New York: Houghton Mifflin, 1959.

Wiget, Andrew. "His Life in His Tail: The Native American Trickster and the Literature of Possibility." In *Redefining American Literature History*, edited by A. LaVonne Brown, Ruoff A. Ward, and Jerry W. Ward. New York: MLA Press, 1990.

Witcher, Esther. "Territorial Newspapers." *Chronicles of Oklahoma* 29 (1951): 484–97.

Wright, J. Leitch. *Creeks and Seminoles*. Lincoln: University of Nebraska Press, 1986.

Zumwalt, Rosemary Levy, ed. *American Folklore Scholarship*. Bloomington: Indiana University Press, 1988.

INDEX

Allen, Paula Gunn, on
  biculturalism, 94; on humor,
  91; on literary tradition, 98; on
  storytelling, 96
animals, communicating with
  humans, 69; social order of,
  67; talking, 6–7, 67–69, 70
Asudi (Cherokee storyteller),
  75–76

Babcock, Barbara, on metanarrative
  elements, 5
Bacone Indian University,
  curriculum at, 2; origin of, 2;
  Posey at, 2. See also *B. I. U.
  Instructor*
Bauman, Richard, and performance
  theory, 5
Benedict, John D., as superinten-
  dent of Indian schools, 10, 11
B. I. U. Instructor, Posey's work
  on, 2
Briggs, Charles L., and performance
  theory, 5
Burns, Robert, 1, 3, 93; influence
  on Posey's work, 54–56, 94;
  "To a Mountain Daisy," 55–56

characters in Fus Fixico letters,
  Choela, 82–83; Fus, 7, 81–83,

86, 91; Hotgun, 7, 18, 24, 26,
  48–49, 50, 80–81, 83–92, 97,
  98; Kono Harjo, 4, 24, 18, 48,
  80, 83, 84, 85, 97; Tookpafka
  Micco, 7, 18, 24, 25–26, 49,
  80, 81, 83–92, 97; Wolf
  Warrior, 4, 18, 48, 80, 83, 84,
  85, 97
characters in verbal tradition,
  Chinnubbie, 4, 51–52, 71–72,
  73–75, 77, 97; Cricket, 69–70;
  Dog, 67–68; Man-eater (Lion),
  7; Opossum, 6, 69–70, 76, 77,
  80; Owl, 4, 67–68, 71–72,
  74–75; Rabbit, 6, 7, 51–53, 57;
  Skunk, 6, 69–70, 76, 77, 80;
  Waboxie Harjo, 51; Woetcoh
  Micco, 51; Wolf, 52–53
Chesnutt, Charles, 95, 98
Chitto Harjo, 16, 18; on
  assimilation, 17. *See also* Crazy
  Snake
Crazy Snake, in Fus Fixico letters,
  91; poem about, 16, 17, 33. *See
  also* Chitto Harjo
Creeks, and assimilation, 10;
  attitude toward blacks, 11;
  education, 10, 11; and
  excessive individualism, 70;
  literacy among, 10; National

Creeks, and assimilation *(cont.)*
Council, 11; removal to Indian
Territory, 9, 10; slavery, 11;
tribal government, 11; verbal
art, 65–77
Creek verbal stories, "How Rabbit
Won His Wife's Sister for His
Second Wife," 53–54; "The
Man Who Became a Snake,"
65; "Rabbit Brags to Man-
eater," 7; "Rabbit Steals Fire,"
65

Dawes Act, 9, 14, 24; Creek reac-
tion to, 15, 17
Deloria, Vine, 79, 85, 92. *See also*
humor

Eastman, Charles A., 47
Eddleman Reed, Ora, 21–22, 60,
94; compared to Alex Posey
and Charles Gibson, 27, 28,
30, 31; "Types of Indian
Girls," 29–30; "What the
Curious Want to Know," 27–29
The Empire Writes Back, 6
este charte, 26–27, 30, 102–3 n. 6.
ethnography, 6
ethnopoetics, defined, 5
Eufaula Indian Journal, Gibson's
writings for, 22–27, 31, 80, 99;
merger with *Eufaula Gazette*,
22; Posey's purchase of, 18;
Posey's work for, 2

five southeastern nations, 42; and
Christianity, 10; and education,
10; and farming (agrarian

systems), 11, 12; government
of, 11; and slavery, 12
Fus Fixico letters. *See under* Alex
Posey, works of

Gibson, Charles, 21, 93, 94;
compared to Ora Eddleman
Reed and Alex Posey, 27, 28,
30, 31; in Fus Fixico letters,
90; response to Fus Fixico
letters, 24–27; writings in
Eufaula Indian Journal,
22–27
Grayson, George W., 14, 23, 25

Harte, Bret, compared to Alex
Posey, 95
humor, in Fus Fixico letters,
80–92; Gerald Vizenor on, 83;
Indian-Euroamerican relations
and, 85–92; James Welch on,
85; Louis Littlecoon Oliver on,
79–80; as mirror of Indian life,
92; Paula Gunn Allen on, 91;
Sigmund Freud on, 86; Vine
Deloria on, 79, 85, 92

Indian, critique of the term, 19
Indian Removal Act of 1830, 9,
10

Krupat, Arnold, on monologic
and dialogic voices, 6

literacy. *See under* Creeks
Littlefield, Daniel F., biography of
Posey, 3, 6
local color, 95, 96

Mooney, James, 67, 72–73
Muskogee Times, 80; Posey's
  purchase of, 15, 18

National Council. *See under*
  Creeks

Oliver, Louis Littlecoon, 65;
  Chasers of the Sun, 66–67,
  68–69; on Indians and humor,
  79–80
Ortiz, Simon, on the colonial
  experience, 22, 97; on
  storytelling, 7

performance theory, 5, 7, 65
Porter, Pleasant, response to
  Dawes Act, 14–15
Posey, Alex, at Bacone Indian
  University, 2; biographical
  information about, 14, 15–16; on
  the capture and imprisonment
  of Crazy Snake, 16, 17;
  compared to Bret Harte, 95;
  compared to Charles Gibson
  and Ora Eddleman Reed, 27,
  28, 30, 31; compared to Mark
  Twain, 95; conflicting
  ideologies in his works, 20, 33;
  at *Eufaula Indian Journal*, 2;
  influence of Henry David
  Thoreau, 4, 33–35, 36, 37–38,
  39, 42, 48, 49, 50; influence of
  other writers, 3, 54; influence
  of Robert Burns, 1, 2, 54–56,
  94; reaction to allotment,
  16–17, 23; reaction to Dawes
  Act, 15, 17, 24; rendering of

black characters, 56–63;
  rendering of black dialect, 56,
  57, 59, 60, 61, 62; response to
  "Rifle Shots," 25–27; use of
  animals in works, 6, 7
Posey Alex, works of, "Bob
  White." 34–35; "The Call of
  the Wild," 37–38;
  "Chinnubbie and the Owl,"
  66, 70–72, 96, 97; "A Creek
  Fable," 65; "Fable of the
  Foolish Bear," 65; Fus Fixico
  letters, 2, 3, 7, 9, 18, 22–27,
  80–92, 94, 96, 97; "Hotgun on
  the Death of Yadeka Harjo,"
  48–50, 94; "The Indians Past
  Olympic," 42–46, "Mose and
  Richard," 4, 56, 60–62, 95;
  "An Outcast," 48, 94; "The
  'Possum and the Skunk,"
  69–70, 96, 97; "To the Crow,"
  35–36; "Tulledega," 38–40,
  42, 94; "Uncle Dick's Sow," 4,
  56, 57–60, 62, 94, 95; "When
  Molly Blows the Dinnerhorn,"
  36–37
Posey, Lewis Henderson,
  "Hence," 1, 2, 54
Posey, Nancy, 1, 6, 51, 52
postcolonialism, as literary theory,
  6

"Red English." *See* este charte
Roosevelt, Theodore, parodied in
  Fus Fixico letters, 89–90

Silko, Leslie Marmon, on
  storytelling, 73–74, 76–77, 82

Siquanid (Cherokee storyteller), 72

slavery, and assimilation, 12; and intermarriage, 12; Posey on, 13, 14; and "state negroes," 12, 13. *See also under* five southeastern nations

Smith, Henry Nash, 11, 13

storytelling, appropriate times for, 70–71; as cultural indicator, 65–77; and individualism, 70; and interweaving of stories, 75–76; and narrators, 73; and ownership of stories, 72; and relationship to Indian culture, 65–77; Simon Ortiz on, 7, 22; and tribal cohesion, 76; and tribal identity, 77

Swanton, John R., on storytelling, 67–68, 69, 70, 72

Tedlock, Dennis, 5

Thoreau, Henry David, 93; compared to Alex Posey, 33–35, 36, 37–38, 39, 42, 45–46, 48, 49, 50; *Journal*, 34, 41; *Maine Woods*, 39–40, 46; recording Indian culture, 34; views on Indian culture, 40–41; *Walden*, 34, 36

tribal newspapers, Cherokee, 10. See also *Eufaula Indian Journal; Muskogee Times; Twin Territories*

Twain, Mark, compared to Alex Posey, 95

Twin Territories, 21, 27, 29, 30, 60, 65, 95, 96

verbal art, Charles Briggs on, 5; description of by Dennis Tedlock, 5, 65, 66. *See also under* Creeks

Vizenor, Gerald, 83. *See also* humor

Welch, James. *See under* humor

Whitman, Walt, 3, 18–19, 54

Zitkala-Ša, 95

Zuni storytelling, relation to Creek storytelling, 70–71